CONTENTS

8 Contents

DENNETT
AND
RICOEUR
ON THE
NARRATIVE SELF

Also available in Contemporary Studies in Philosophy and the Human Sciences

Series Editors: Hugh J. Silverman and Graeme Nicholson

DENNETT

AND

RICOEUR

ON THE

NARRATIVE SELF

JOAN
McCARTHY

Humanity
Books

an imprint of Prometheus Books
59 John Glenn Drive, Amherst, New York 14228-2119

Inquiries should be addressed to
Humanity Books
59 John Glenn Drive
Amherst, New York 14228-2119
VOICE: 716-691-0133, ext. 210
FAX: 716-691-0137
WWW.PROMETHEUSBOOKS.COM

11 10 09 08   5 4 3 2

Library of Congress Cataloging-in-Publication Data

McCarthy, Joan.
    Dennett and Ricoeur on the narrative self / by Joan McCarthy.
        p. cm.
    Includes bibliographical references.
    ISBN: 13 978-1-59102-548-1
    1. Self (Philosophy) 2. Dennett, Daniel Clement. 3. Ricoeur, Paul.
4. Naturalism. I. Title.

BD450.M346 2007
126.09'2—dc22   2007011183

ACKNOWLEDGMENTS

My sincere thanks to Dolores Dooley for her many years of collegial support and friendship, and for her careful and critical scrutiny of early drafts of the entire manuscript. Thanks, too, to a number of people who read various chapters and deepened my understanding of the problems I was wrestling with: Tony O'Connor, Matthew Ratcliffe, and Hugh Silverman. I have also been blessed with the good will of family and friends. I would like to express my gratitude to them all, but especially Sara Wilbourne for her unflinching faith in me, Bernie McCarthy for her steadfast support, and Patricia and Killian O'Dwyer for their love.

*I dedicate this book to the memory of my parents,
Maudie O'Reilly and Christy McCarthy.*

Introduction

WHY THE
NARRATIVE SELF?

The aim of this book is to consider a positive alternative to traditional views of the human self understood either as a kind of real thing or as an illusion. I suggest that the self is best conceived as neither real nor illusory, but as a culturally mediated narrative unity of action, and I support this view by drawing on the work of two contemporary philosophers, Daniel Dennett and Paul Ricoeur. Their positions are of particular interest because, while they work within different philosophical traditions, analytic and continental philosophy respectively, both theorists cast the self in narrative terms.

CONTEMPORARY INTEREST IN NARRATIVE

Almost all human beings narrate, or tell stories, as a way of communicating information and making sense of experiences. The word *narrative*, itself, refers to two kinds of activities—telling and knowing—and derives from the Latin terms *narrö* (meaning "relate, tell") from the original Sanskrit root *gnâ* (meaning "know") and *gnärus* (meaning "knowing, acquainted with, expert, skilful").[1] Traditionally, the humanities and social sciences have understood the narrative as a form of communication, a rich source of qualitative data about the lives and worlds of people as told by personal accounts and biographies. More recently, the relationship between narrative and knowledge has been highlighted, and the process of narration is increasingly seen as a means of making human lives intelligible. This is particularly the case in three related disciplines—psychoanalysis, history, and philosophy.[2]

Building on Freud's deployment of the narrative in analysis and case-studies, psychologists like Donald Polkinghorne and Bruner have promoted the usefulness of the narrative method as a means of understanding the way in which the self is psychologically constructed and constituted. Polkinghorne describes the narrative as a "cognitive organizing process" and the self as a "temporal Gestalt" where the meaning of individual life events and actions is determined not by the characteristics or abilities they might exhibit, but by their relationship with the whole to a unified story with a particular plot or theme.[3] Jerome Bruner distinguishes between two modes of thinking: the logico-scientific mode, which he calls the paradigmatic mode, and the narrative mode.[4] The former concerns itself with description and explanation; its tools are those of conceptualization and categorization, and the disciplines associated with it are mathematics, logic, and the natural sciences. While the paradigmatic mode seeks to generalize, the narrative mode focuses on the particular in order to understand the meaning of experiences as unique historical and personal events. The narrative mode leads, for Bruner, to "good stories, gripping drama, believable (though not necessarily 'true') historical accounts."[5] In describing the operation of narration as a means of understanding individual lives (in addition to being a means of simply recounting them), Polkinghorne and Bruner underline the role of narration as a mode of intelligibility. This, in turn, raises the issue of the relationship, if any, between narrative accounts and historical accounts of human lives. The nature of the relationship between narrative and personal history is the focus of much of recent psychological literature. In particular, the question of whether the primary aim of analysis is to render the experiences and memories of the analysand into a meaningful coherent story, or to retrieve past events from repression and the distortions of memory, is the subject of debate.[6] (This concern is of particular interest to philosophy, and I explore it in more detail in chapter 6.)

The view of narrative as a mode of understanding has also been the subject of much debate in historical theory.[7] Traditionally, the narratives told by historians have been considered truthful to the extent that they tell the stories of real people and actual events in the past. This view distinguishes between historical narratives and literary narratives on the grounds that the latter generally refer to imaginary figures and events.

Increasingly, however, the relationship between historical narrative accounts and the reality they purport to describe has been questioned. Three important positions have emerged. First, the narrative as a mode of explanation is considered to be deeply suspect, unstable, and inadequate by those who see history as a science. On this view, even though historical narratives may refer to actual events, the way in which these events are structured or ordered according to the narrative form results in their distortion. The scientific approach sees the proper task of history as the explanation of human behavior and events in terms of general laws that are causal and nonteleological.[8] A second view, associated with French poststructuralist thinkers such as Roland Barthes, Michel Foucault, and Jacques Derrida, also treats the historical narrative with suspicion, but not because of its unscientific status. Barthes, for example, challenges the distinction between historical narrative, conceived as real, and fictional narrative such as epics, novels, and dramas, conceived as imaginary.[9] What is imaginary for Barthes about narrative representation is not its association with literature, but rather the illusion it fosters that there can be a privileged narrator looking at and apprehending the processes of the world. On this view, a narrative mode of explanation is not especially privileged and is simply one discourse among others, which is itself historically and culturally embedded. A third view, held by analytic theorists such as Hayden White, Arthur Danto, Louis Mink, and continental thinkers such as Hans-Georg Gadamer and Paul Ricoeur, consider that the narrative form is particularly appropriate to understanding human events.[10] This is because they view human action as purposive, goal-oriented, and enacted over time. Thus they conclude that human events are best understood as parts of a whole story with a temporal structure of beginning, middle, and end. In sum, this position holds that the form of the historical narrative mirrors the form of human life.

Concerns about the relationship between narration and knowledge that arise in psychoanalysis and history have also been raised in philosophy. Reading and telling of stories has always played an important role in philosophical enquiry—think of Plato's deployment of myth; Humean, Lockean, or Parfitian puzzle-cases; the contemporary revival of interest in casuistry as a teaching tool in bioethics; or Martha Nussbaum's thesis that reading literature develops moral sensibilities.[11] In addition to its traditional deployment in philosophical analysis, however, the role of the narrative and its contribution to the refinement and solution of philosophical problems has been expanded in recent years. The publication, for example, of Hannah Arendt's *Human Condition* in 1958 marked a shift in the philosophical role, which the narrative had hitherto played in philosophy toward a conception of the narrative as a representative form for human lives:

> That every individual life between birth and death can
> eventually be told as a story with beginning and end is
> the prepolitical and prehistorical condition of history,
> the great story without beginning and end. But the
> reason why each human life tells its story and why his-
> tory ultimately becomes the storybook of mankind,

with many actors and speakers and yet without any
tangible authors, is that both are the outcome of
action.[12]

More recently, a number of philosophers from both analytic and continental traditions have constructed theories of the self and accounts of personal identity on the
basis of comparisons that they have drawn between the
form of the narrative and the form of individual human
lives. Amongst others, Daniel Dennett, Owen Flanagan,
Alasdair MacIntyre, Paul Ricoeur, Charles Taylor, and Margaret Urban Walker have made significant contributions
to debates on the philosophical significance of narrative
explanation for self-understanding. Importantly, while
there are deep divisions and differences among their
positions, all of these philosophers reject the traditional
account of the self as some kind of thing or substance.
Instead, they claim the unity and continuity of the self
over time is based on a narrative ordering.

IS THE SELF REAL OR ILLUSORY?

The idea that the self is a kind of entity that can be conceived in different ways—traditionally as a substance or,
currently, as a narrative unity—raises the question of the
ontological status of the self.[13] In other words, to what, if
anything, do concepts of the self refer? Even a very brief
foray into the philosophical literature on the concept of
self reveals that there is no consensus as to its
meaning.[14] It has been taken to mean some kind of

inner unity or mental presence, but it has also been defined as simply the form of the body, or a set of unique character traits or origin of action. With the exception of Plato, the early Greeks and Aristotle, in particular, claimed that the self represented the breath of life in the body and was intrinsic to it. More recently, Galen Strawson, echoing Descartes, starts from the fact that people have a sense of themselves as a kind of mental presence or thing that is single over time, or a conscious subject of experience that is distinct from all particular experiences.[15] Alternatively, Kathleen Wilkes construes the self in terms of psychological dispositions, time-related emotions such as guilt, and practices such as planning for a future.[16]

It follows that the problem of determining the conditions of the unity and continuity of the self translates into several problems, depending on the content that is ascribed to the term self (that is, assumptions about what the self is), that shape the kinds of questions that can be asked about its unity (at any one time) and continuity (over time).

When philosophers have sought to describe the *nature* of the self—whatever it is that the concept of the self refers to (however fuzzy)—they have generally concluded that either the self is "real" in the sense that it has a fixed nature of some kind (it is a material or immaterial substance) or that there is no self at all (either it is an illusion or at best a theoretical abstraction, a sociological construction, or a product of language).

Granted the confusion and the disagreement, the concept of self is increasingly described as a "philosophical muddle" or a "piece of philosophical jargon" that doesn't do much to explain human experience and behavior, and the temptation is there to dispense with it altogether.[17] Even so, the narrative self, as a recent arrival to the collection of possible models of the self, is on the whole, I will argue, a better candidate for the work that selves purport to do than its more traditional rivals. Two different but related theories of the narrative self are worth serious consideration: Dennett's naturalist account and Ricoeur's phenomenological-hermeneutic account.

There is a range of different naturalist positions in philosophy; so, for my purposes, I associate naturalism with the analytic philosophical tradition and define it as a philosophical approach which assumes that nature forms a mind-independent unity best described and explained in terms of the objective, third-person perspective and methodologies of the natural sciences. As I show in chapter 1, contemporary naturalist positions differ in the importance of the role they assign to the language of the self in explanations of human behavior. For example, for Paul Churchland, the explanation of human mental processes will eventually be best achieved in terms of the language and methodologies of neuroscience rather than psychology. On his account, psychological concepts such as beliefs, attitudes, desires, and selves can be dispensed with in the longer term. Alternatively, for Daniel Dennett, a useful concept of self can be drawn in terms of a particular account of consciousness and a consideration of evolutionary theory. He describes such a self as a theoretical fiction and argues that, developments in neuroscience aside, the self remains, and always will remain, a useful tool in the explanation and prediction of human behavior.

There are as many different phenomenological-hermeneutic philosophical positions as there are naturalist; so, for my purposes, I understand it as a continental philosophical approach, which, inspired by Edmund Husserl, rejects the objectivist stance of naturalism. Husserl's strategy is to bracket what he describes as the naïve assumption that there is a mind-independent reality that can be made intelligible by the natural sciences. Instead, he argues that what is real, if anything can be described as real, is the world of individual experience within which humans live and construct realms of meaning. More recent interpretations of Husserl's enterprise, such as those of Maurice Merleau-Ponty and Paul Ricoeur, view any given experience as mediated through historically embedded socio-cultural frameworks. In short, contemporary continental approaches, in general, eschew scientific explanation in favor of historical and cultural contextualization.

As I explain in chapter 5, Ricoeur, as a continental philosopher, understands the human being not as an object of investigation whose features can be adequately explained in terms of the methods and standards of the natural sciences, but as a unique origin of action. On his view, activities (for example, acting, speaking, and recounting) can be taken as, more properly, human modes of existence that are pre-scientific and historically embedded. From this theoretical background, he casts the concept of self as narrated, as a *character*—a culturally mediated unity based on a narrative order that represents basic features of human existence.

Although Dennett and Ricoeur come at the notion of
the self from two different traditions, their positions are
similar in a number of key ways. First, they are both suspicious of traditional notions of the self as a mental object
of some kind. Second, in spite of their suspicions, they
both refuse to view the self solely in material terms—as a
location in the brain—and they each seek to maintain
some kind of a distinction between psychological language and the language of the brain sciences. Finally, they
both conclude that the preferred way of viewing the
problem of the unity and continuity of the self is to cast
the self in narrative terms. Thus, the concept of the narrative self stands on the faultline between naturalist (analytic) and phenomenological-hermeneutic (continental)
philosophies, and Dennett and Ricoeur are its mediators.
By this I mean that Dennett mediates between science
and life, Ricoeur between literature and life. Dennett, for
example, explains the narrative self by appealing to such
things as computers, mathematical abstractions, and evolutionary predispositions. Alternatively, Ricoeur's understanding of the narrative self draws on literary characters,
tragic plot lines, and psychoanalytic phenomena. A central aim of this book is to assess the merits of these competing narrative approaches with a view to sketching a
plausible account of narrative selfhood.

NOTES TO INTRODUCTION

1. Hayden White, *The Content of the Form: Narrative Discourse and Historical Representation* (Baltimore and

London: The John Hopkins University Press, 1987), pp. 1, 215, fn.2.

2. Of course, the humanities, in general, have paid a lot of attention to the activity of telling stories. In literature, for example, novels, plays, and epic poems have traditionally been analyzed in part on the basis of their narrative structure. That is, individual events within a novel or play are explained in terms of their role in the whole of the story, in particular, in terms of their relation to its beginning, middle, or end. See Frank Kermode, *The Sense of an Ending: Studies in the Theory of Fiction* (London: Oxford University Press, 1966) for an analysis of the role of narrative in literature. See also Daniel Albright, "Literary and Psychological Models of the Self," in *The Remembering Self, Construction and Accuracy in the Self-Narrative*, ed. Ulric Neisser and Robyn Fivush (Cambridge: Cambridge University Press, 1994), pp. 19–39, for an overview of contemporary treatments of narrative form.

3. Donald E. Polkinghorne, "Narrative and Self-Concept," *Journal of Narrative and Life History* 1, nos. 2 and 3 (1991): 135–153.

4. Jerome Bruner, *Actual Minds, Possible Worlds* (Cambridge, MA: Harvard University Press, 1986), p. 101.

5. For Bruner, the narrative mode "deals in human or human-like intention and action and the vicissitudes and consequences that mark their course. It strives to put its timeless miracles into the particulars of experience, and to locate the experience in time and place" (ibid., p. 13).

6. For more on this, see Donald P. Spence, "Narrative Appeal vs Historical Validity," *Contemporary Psychoanalysis* 25, no. 3 (1989): 517–24; "Narrative Persuasion," *Psychoanalysis and Contemporary Thought* 6, no. 3 (1983): 457–81; and *Narrative Truth and Historical Truth* (New York: W. W. Norton & Co., 1982). See also M. Eagle, "Psychoanalysis and

'Narrative Truth': A Reply to Spence," *Psychoanalysis and Contemporary Thought* 7, no. 4 (1984): 629–40; and Dan P. Mc Adams, "Introductory Commentary," *Journal of Narrative and Life History* 5, no. 3 (1995): 207–211.

7. See White, *The Content of the Form*, chapter 2, for an overview of different views of the status of the narrative in historical theory from the past three decades.

8. One example of this position is that of the French *Annales* group, associated with Ferdinand Braudel, who viewed narrative historiography as a non-scientific, even ideological form of representation. Note that causal explanations explain any event or entity (*e*) in terms of events or entities antecedent to (*e*), while teleological explanations (from the Greek word *telos*, meaning "goal, task, completion") explains an event or entity (*e*) in terms of its contribution to an ideal state, normal functioning, and the achievement of goals of organizations or wholes (such as stories) that they belong to.

9. Roland Barthes, *Image, Music, Text* (Glasgow: Fontana/Collins, 1977), pp. 79–124.

10. White, *The Content of the Form*; Arthur C. Danto, *Narration and Knowledge* (New York: Columbia University Press, 1985); Louis Mink, "Narrative Form as a Cognitive Instrument," in *The Writing of History: Literary Form and Historical Understanding*, ed. Robert H. Canary and Henry Kozicki (Madison, WI: Madison Press), pp. 143–44; Hans-Georg Gadamer, *Truth and Method* (London: Sheed & Ward, 1975); and chapters 4, 5, and 6 of this book.

11. For further discussion of the benefits of the role of narrative in ethical reasoning, see the concluding chapter of this book.

12. Hannah Arendt, *The Human Condition* (Chicago: University of Chicago Press, 1958), p. 184.

13. I use the concepts of *self* and *person* interchangeably. It

might be argued that the *self* is more properly construed as some kind of internal unity or faculty, and that the term *person* more closely describes an entity who can be considered morally accountable. However, I think that the notions are sufficiently interrelated to warrant their equivalence and further that not to do so here would lead to confusion because the philosophers I am engaging with, Dennett and Ricoeur, make no distinction between them. For an elaboration of the notion of the self, see Galen Strawson, "The Self," *Journal of Consciousness Studies* 4, nos. 5–6 (1997): 405–28 and "The Self and the Sesmet," *Journal of Consciousness Studies* 6, no. 4 (1999): 99–135.

14. When I deploy the term *concept of the self*, I do not mean to imply by the placement of the definite article before *self* that the latter is a single count noun, nor that I am referring to some kind of generic *self* in the same way as I might refer to a table or mountain. Therefore, when I use *concept of the self,* take it to mean *concept of self* and know that I make no pre-theoretical commitments as to what *self* might turn out to be. The same applies to my deployment of the concept of *the narrative self*.

15. Strawson, "The Self," pp. 405–28; and "The Self and the Sesmet," pp. 99–135.

16. Kathleen Wilkes, "Know Thyself," *Journal of Consciousness Studies* 5, no. 2 (1998): 153–65; and *Real People* (Oxford: Clarendon Press, 1994).

17. In a 1998 article aptly titled "There is No Problem of the Self," *Journal of Consciousness Studies* 5, nos. 5–6 (1998): 645–57, Eric T. Olson describes "the self" as a piece of "philosophical jargon [. . .] masquerading as ordinary language" (p. 646). See also *Models of the Self*, ed. Shaun Gallagher and Jonathan Shear (New York: Imprint Academic, 1999) for an edited collection of articles on contemporary accounts of the self.

Chapter One

DENNETT'S BRAND OF NATURALISM

Daniel Dennett declares his philosophical starting point as "the objective, materialistic, third-person world of the physical sciences."[1] He is, first and foremost, a naturalist philosopher who approaches the explanation of any given phenomenon with the assumption that a mind-independent realm exists and that it can be made intelligible, more or less successfully, by empiricist methodologies. Specifically, in relation to the ontological status of psychological phenomena (beliefs, intentions, desires, minds, selves), Dennett describes himself as a "mild realist" in order to distinguish his position from a number of other possible philosophical responses to the problem of the relationship between the mental and the physical.[2] His adoption of a mild-realist position is based on his desire to hold on to a scientific realist perspective of the world—where what is real is determined by science—while at the same time retain a role for talk about mental states, beliefs, and selves without reducing the latter to the former.

To do this, Dennett distinguishes his position from what he calls Jerry Fodor's "industrial strength Realism," from Paul Churchland's "eliminative materialism," and from Richard Rorty's "milder-than-mild irrealism."[3] For Dennett, "Fodor's industrial strength Realism takes beliefs to be things in the head—just like cells and blood vessels and viruses."[4] Even so, he refuses to concede that a rejection of Fodor's position renders psychological postulates meaningless and entails a commitment to an eliminative materialist position such as that of Churchland.[5]

Specifically, while Dennett agrees with Churchland that "beliefs are quite real enough to call real" as long as they can successfully predict human behavior, he disagrees with Churchland's further claim that psychological language can, in principle, and will, in time, be replaced by the language of the brain sciences.[6] For Dennett, the benefits of greater explanatory and predictive success would, likely, be outweighed by the difficulties involved in using the cumbersome system that he anticipates neuroscience would produce. In addition, its sheer size would increase its exposure to error. He concludes that Churchland's prognosis for the brain sciences is based on a "hunch" that, even if realized, would not entail the replacement of psychological language with the supposedly "superior" language of the brain sciences.[7] Finally he distinguishes his position from that of Richard Rorty on the grounds that he (Dennett) can test the intelligibility of different kinds of claims (such as the different claims of psychology and astrology) on the basis of their explanatory and predictive success. Rorty's position for Dennett cannot permit this distinction to be validly made, and while he admits to agreeing with Rorty on several fronts, he acknowledges that he is "still quite conservative in [his] adoption of Standard Scientific Epistemology and Metaphysics."[8]

In brief, Dennett's thesis is that there is something intrinsic to the human organism that correlates to some degree with psychological language, but that this something cannot be understood by crudely postulating brain structures mapping on to psychological concepts. Instead, he argues the correlation is best expressed by adopting different third-person stances in order to explain human experience and behavior.

THE HETEROPHENOMENOLOGICAL METHOD (HM)

Granted his privileging of the third-person perspective combined with his endeavor to make a place for psychological language in understanding human behavior, Dennett's mild realist brand of naturalism leads him to develop what he calls the "heterophenomenological method" (HM).[9] In *Consciousness Explained* (*CE*), and elsewhere, Dennett outlines four features of the HM as it is applied to the phenomenon of consciousness.[10] The first feature of the HM is that it describes the "heterophenomenological world" (HW) of human subjects as expressed by them through verbal reports of their conscious experience. The second is that it records the subject's behavioral reactions, hormonal and visceral responses, and other physically detectable changes.

> We start with recorded raw data. Among these are the
> vocal sounds people make (what they say, in other
> words), but to these verbal reports must be added all
> the other manifestations of belief, conviction, expecta-
> tion, fear, loathing, disgust, etc., including any and all
> internal conditions (e.g., brain activities, hormonal dif-
> fusion, heart rate changes, etc.) detectable by objec-
> tive means.[11]

The third feature of the HM is that it carries out its description of subjects' reports of their experience without prejudging whether or not these subjects are liars, zombies (unconscious ghouls who just look like regular conscious folk), or computers: "The heterophe-nomenological method neither challenges nor accepts as entirely true the assertions of subjects, but rather maintains a constructive and sympathetic neutrality, in the hopes of compiling a definitive description of the world according to the subjects."[12] This third feature, he claims, is similar to the Husserlian *epoché* in that it describes the phenomena of conscious experience without prejudging their ontological status.[13]

The fourth feature of the HM is its adoption of one of three possible third-person stances to explain the experience and behavior of the subject concerned. Of the latter, Dennett claims that the "intentional stance" is the most relevant.

> Here's how it [the intentional stance] works: first you
> decide to treat an object whose behavior is to be pre-
> dicted as a rational agent; then you figure out what
> beliefs that agent ought to have, given its place in the

world and its purpose. Then you figure out what desires it ought to have, on the same considerations, and finally you predict that this rational agent will act to further its goals in the light of its beliefs. A little practical reasoning from the chosen set of beliefs and desires will in many—but not all—instances yield a decision about what the agent ought to do; that is what you predict the agent *will* do.[14]

For example, how is my current behavior (sustained research and furious typing) to be explained? The intentional stance would attribute to me a desire to succeed as a professional philosopher, a belief that work of this nature will ensure same, and an additional belief that there is a persisting self who will be the future beneficiary of my present toil. The intentional stance is successful for Dennett, not because it tells us something about the content of real brains or about consciousness or subjective experience, but because it has predictive power. Other third-person strategies are the physical stance and the design stance. For example, the wear and tear on the keys of the computer might best be explained by Dennett in terms of the physical stance, which would involve viewing me as one kind of physical object impacting on another. Or again, the spread and dexterity of my fingers as I type might be explained in terms of my place in an evolutionary continuum (the design stance).

To recap, the HM approaches the analysis of first-person conscious experience in four different ways:

1. gathering the data of first-person reports of their experience
2. observing subjects' emotional and physiological reactions
3. bracketing any worries about the ontological status of the objects of conscious experience
4. taking a third-person stance toward the subjects concerned

Dennett posits the HM as an alternative to other naturalist solutions to the problem of relating psychological language and the language of the brain sciences, the mental and physical, the mind and brain. As indicated, it is his attempt to hold on to both languages without reducing the psychological to the neurophysiological. However, the question that arises is whether or not the HM offers a consistent and coherent approach to explaining human experience and behavior. In effect, while it differs from the usual scientific solutions such as behaviorism or eliminative materialism, the four features of the HM seem only nominally related with one another and one is left with the dizzying sense that each one of these features yields very different standards against which one can measure one's theoretical progress. While the first feature values first-person reports, the second feature ensures that these are placed alongside the publicly accessible data of physiology and biology and the latter are trumped over the former. Dennett justifies this second feature on the grounds that "all Cartesian or 'first-person perspective' starting points lure the theorist into . . . creating whole genres of bogus *data* for the theorist to stumble over."[15] Because human subjects confabulate, guess, speculate, and theorize, Dennett, like Descartes, is concerned that the first-person perspective, on its own, is an "incubator of errors" and "at best an uncertain guide" to what is actually going on in human subjects.[16] And his response, also like that of Descartes, is to place first-person reports "within the fold of standard scientific ('third-person') data," in other words, to combine first-person reports with other publicly accessible data such as observable physiological responses.[17]

Again, while the third feature explicitly brackets drawing any ontological inferences about the status of the heterophenomenological phenomena of the HW, this is difficult to maintain, given that Dennett insists that non-phenomenological features such as bodies and brains trump the HW. At one stage, for example, Dennett asks: "[w]hat would it be to confirm subjects' beliefs in their own phenomenology?" and concludes:[18]

> My suggestion, then, is that if we were to find real goings-on in people's brains that had enough of the "defining" properties of the items that populate their heterophenomenological worlds, we could reasonably propose that we had discovered what they were really talking about—even if they initially resisted the identifications. And if we discovered that the real goings-on bore only a minor resemblance to the heterophenomenological items, we could reasonably declare that people were just mistaken in the beliefs they expressed, in spite of their sincerity.[19]

For Dennett, the means of deciding what subjects are "really talking about" is to discover the "real goings-on in people's brains" and this is done, not on the authority of the subjects themselves (who may be sincere but mistaken) but by appealing to the authority of the objectivist approach.

Finally, it is difficult to see how the fourth feature can be reconciled with the other three. It involves the adoption of a third-person stance toward the subject in question, but there don't seem to be any prima facie reasons why one kind of stance should trump another (e.g., the design over the intentional), nor is it clear how the other three features might help us to decide.

CONSCIOUSNESS AND THE SELF

Granted that there are serious difficulties with Dennett's brand of naturalism, specifically the HM, it is, nevertheless, worthwhile taking a closer look at how Dennett applies it as a means of construing consciousness and, by implication, the self. Traditionally, Cartesian-inspired accounts of the nature of human beings construe the self as significantly related to the phenomenon of consciousness. The aim of this strategy has been to provide a basis for understanding the self as a single, stable, persisting entity of some kind: a *res cogitans* or thinking thing. Dennett also understands the self in relation to consciousness but, as already indicated, he analyzes consciousness within the terms of his naturalistic strategy. What distinguishes his approach from a Cartesian one is that, unlike

Descartes, Dennett argues that the self, as it is usually regarded, is a fiction because, among other things, consciousness, on which it supposedly relies, is fragmented, unstable, and discontinuous.

On Dennett's account, the fact that human beings are capable of conscious thought has traditionally led philosophers and scientists to conclude that wherever there is a conscious mind, there is a point of view or observer who takes in a limited amount of the available information on any given space-time continuum. For practical purposes, "we can consider the point of view of a particular conscious subject to be just that: *a point* moving through space-time."[20] Dennett argues, however, that mistakes have been made when theorists have attempted to describe and locate such a point of view as a point within the individual. Difficulties with description and location have prompted two different, but related Cartesian-inspired solutions.

First, the Cartesian dualist thesis suggests that the possibility of having conscious thoughts, or a point of view, implies that these are properties of a *res cogitans*, or thinking thing.[21] Further, it describes this thinking thing as a self, the controller of the body and the will; the originator of intentions and plans; and the seat of personality, beliefs, values, and memory. Finally, it claims that if such a thinking thing cannot be located in the physical body, it must be an immaterial substance that interacts with the body in some way.[22] Having set out the moves involved in Cartesian dualism, Dennett quickly aligns himself with the traditional refutation that is associated with Gilbert Ryle—briefly, that it fails to explain the operations of consciousness because it places the subject of consciousness at a further remove. Simply put, the dualist account of consciousness ends up with an observer within an observer, a ghost within the machine.[23]

Second, the Cartesian materialist view is described by Dennett as the position that one arrives at if one discards Cartesian dualism but fails to discard the imagery of a "central (but material) theater" where events are represented and transduced into conscious thought for appreciation by an audience."[24] The Cartesian materialist view construes the origin of conscious thoughts as a thing-like self and seeks counterparts in the brain for different features of consciousness.[25] On the notion of a Cartesian Theater, Dennett comments,

> There is no such place. Any theory that postulates such a place is still in the grip of Cartesian Materialism. What (and where) is this "I"? It is not an organ, a subfaculty, a place in the brain, a medium—or medium—into which information gets transduced. My attack on the Cartesian Theater is among other things an attack on the very practice . . . of positing unanalyzed "I" or "we" or "self" or "subject" who "has access" to x or y, as if we could take this as a primitive of our theorizing. Any sane account of the mechanisms of consciousness must begin with a denial of Cartesian Materialism; and that leads irresistibly to the view that the "me" has to be constructed out of the interactions, not vice versa.[26]

Dennett's argument is that if Cartesian materialism can be repudiated as an account of what happens with conscious thoughts, then there are implications for the status of the self that are inevitable or irresistible. Without the Cartesian Theater—the place where conscious thoughts come together—the "I" need not be viewed as thing-like, a primitive entity that exists prior to conscious thoughts and manipulates them. Rather, the self is better understood as a phenomenon that is constructed out of the "interactions" of the mechanisms of consciousness. The point is that if the phenomenon of consciousness is redescribed in terms other than the Cartesian Theater—for example, in terms of Dennett's Multiple Draft Model (MDM)—then the concept of the self can be similarly redescribed, in this case, in narrative terms.

Dennett devotes most of *CE* to showing that Cartesian materialism is not a useful way of describing the relationship between the phenomenon of consciousness and the brain. A key objection that Dennett has to Cartesian materialism is that it cannot account for the *dis*continuity of consciousness, which he describes as its most striking feature.[27] On Dennett's account of Cartesian materialism, consciousness is pictured as streamlike: the order of *conscious experiences* of events is construed as mirroring the actual order of these events in the world. However, he argues that the Cartesian model fails to provide a satisfactory explanation for a number of features of consciousness that are important. He demonstrates this through an exploration of a number of puzzle cases such as the color phi phenomenon,[28] the binding problem,[29] and blindsight.[30] The point Dennett is making is that a computational model of the human organism can better explain our cognitive processes than the traditional language of mind and mental states, which privilege introspection and posit a persisting subject of streamlike conscious experiences. Alternatively, Dennett's MDM depicts the mind/brain as a kind of information processor: a parallel distributed processing computer with large networks of simpler processing units that respond to sensory inputs and communicate with one another along neural pathways:[31]

> There is no single, definitive "stream of consciousness," because there is no central headquarters, no Cartesian Theater where "it all comes together" for the perusal of a Central Meaner. Instead of such a single stream (however wide), there are multiple channels in which specialist circuits try, in parallel pandemoniums, to do their various things, creating Multiple Drafts as they go. Most of these fragmentary drafts of "narrative" play short-lived roles in the modulation of current activity but some get promoted to further functional roles, in swift succession, by the activity of a virtual machine in the brain. The seriality of this machine (its "von Neumannesque" character) is not a "hard-wired" design feature, but rather the upshot of a succession of these specialists.[32]

It might be argued that Dennett himself remains faithful to the Cartesian account of consciousness because his deployment of metaphors, such as "draft" and "narrative," presupposes the need for an editor and narrator. On this reading, even the MDM seems to need an "I" to do the important work. However, Dennett can answer such an objection because he does not deny that accounts of subjective experience are edited and revised. Rather, what distinguishes his position from the Cartesian alternative is his claim that these revisions and editions are not always, or even often, the outcome of conscious editorial work. And he deploys metaphors such as "multiple channels" and "narrative fragments" precisely in order to undermine any Cartesian privileging of such editors and narrators.

> On the MDM there is no single place in the brain where information "comes together" for the inspection of the "Central Meaner." Rather there are myriad subsystems generating multiple information states under continuous "editorial revision" and which eventually elicit a behavioral response. This means that there are multiple channels of "narrative fragments" but no "canonical version" or "first edition" that clearly identifies the order of events in the stream of consciousness of the subject.[33]

What Dennett deploys here is a language that can explain cognitive processes in terms that do not privilege a distinction between conscious and nonconscious activity, and he accounts for the effects of consciousness by appealing to unconscious systems: the "myriad subsystems," "multiple information states," and "multiple channels" of the "virtual machine" in the brain.[34]

Accepting the greater explanatory adequacy of the MDM over the Cartesian model with regard to the puzzle cases mentioned above, Dennett can reject the idea that consciousness represents any actual brain states or processes that are available for exploration by scientific methodologies:

> I say that we already know enough empirical facts about what consciousness *isn't* to know that the ordinary concept of consciousness, like the concept of *fatigues*, is too frail; it could never be turned into the sort of scientific concept that could wring answers to the currently unanswerable questions.[35]

Comparing the concept of consciousness with the concept of "fatigues," he describes the latter as a phenomenon that people in an imaginary land have a strange doctrine about: they believe that too many fatigues can spoil one's aim, one fatigue in the legs is worth two in the arm, and they worry about where fatigues go when they are asleep. Dennett's point is that scientists, when confronting this doctrine, cannot appeal to any particular fact of the matter in order to show which theory of fatigues is the right one. The category of fatigues is simply not appropriate to scientific investigation. Similarly, consciousness, on Dennett's account, does not refer to any intrinsic entity: its meaning, "like love and money," depends "to a surprising extent on its associated concepts."[36] What Dennett is rejecting is the notion that consciousness is:

> a property that has sharp boundaries in the brain—and in the world. . . . Consciousness is a cerebral celebrity—nothing more and nothing less. Those contents are conscious that persevere, that monopolize resources long enough to achieve certain typical

and "symptomatic" effects—on memory, on the control of behavior and so forth.[37]

Since *CE* was published, Dennett has developed the idea of consciousness as a "cerebral celebrity," seeing the latter as a useful metaphor because it distances the notion of consciousness even more radically from Cartesian-inspired alternative imagery.[38] The central point for Dennett is that even if it is useful to deploy psychological language to describe some functions of the brain (those that "monopolize resources long enough" or display effects on memory and behavior), what is interesting about these functions, from an explanatory point of view, is not the fact that they are conscious.[39]

There has been a great deal of discussion, praise, and criticism of Dennett's account of consciousness in the intervening years. One core objection to Dennett's thesis is that rather than explaining consciousness, he has explained it away. He has simply avoided what David Chalmers calls the "hard problem" of subjective experience by denying that consciousness is an *explanandum*, and that it exists as a datum any acceptable theory of the mind/brain must account for.[40] For many of the critics of Dennett's position, an account of the behavioral functions of processes like perception or conceptualization is all well and good. But it is not a *sufficient* explanation of why these processes should be accompanied by subjective experience, the experience of "what it is like" to see, think, and talk.[41]

However adequate or inadequate Dennett's model turns out to be as a means of expressing the relationship between consciousness and the brain, my interest in it is of a different order. This is because my project is not directly concerned with Dennett's account of consciousness, but in the implications it has for a construal of the self. Granting, then, that Dennett's MDM captures at least some of the important features of consciousness, my task is to assess the way in which the MDM supports Dennett's conceptualization of the self. Dennett claims that because consciousness can be shown to be a cerebral celebrity—not any kind of entity with distinct boundaries—this implies that any kind of self that is based on it is equally fuzzy. This is his positive thesis, that where Cartesian materialism elicits a concept of the self with strict criteria of identity, the MDM account of consciousness allows for a concept of the self with blurred boundaries. He calls the latter a *center of narrative gravity*, which I will explain in chapter 2.

What emerges from this chapter is a picture of Dennett as a philosopher who attempts to carve out a naturalist approach to psychological phenomena that is objectivist but not reductionist. This is evidenced in his account of the HM, which, however irreconcilable its four features, at least acknowledges that first-person reports of conscious experience have a part to play in any complete account of human life. This is also evident in his naturalized account of consciousness. On the one hand, his account denies that human behavior is the end result of some kind of center of consciousness that is connected with (dualism) or part of (materialism) the physical body of each individual human being. On the other hand, he continues to deploy the term consciousness because he considers it to be theoretically useful, even though he admits that it does not directly refer to any part of the real world (the scientifically determined world).

Given Dennett's brand of naturalism combined with his approach to the phenomenon of consciousness, we are now in a position to examine and evaluate his treatment of the problem of the self. His strategy prompts an interesting question in relation to notions of self: must the ontological parameters—the real nature or extension of concepts of the self—be drawn before anything meaningful can be said about notions of the self? From Dennett's perspective, as we will see, they do not: concern with how real the self is—how (for him) it is related to neurophysiological processes—is not the problem, or at least, it is not the part of the problem that has to be addressed first. His interest in the concept of the self is in determining how *useful* its deployment is in explaining and predicting human behavior. The test for any theorist, on this account, who explains human behavior by deploying a concept of self, is to show that this way of describing behavior enhances our ability to explain it. I investigate and evaluate this thesis in the following two chapters.

NOTES TO CHAPTER 1

1. Daniel Dennett, *The Intentional Stance* (Cambridge, MA: Bradford Books/MIT Press, 1987), p. 5.

2. Daniel Dennett, *Brainchildren* (London: Penguin, 1998), p. 98. Originally published as "Real Patterns," *Journal of Philosophy* 88 (January 1991): 27-51.

3. Ibid., pp. 113–14.

4. Ibid. Fodor argues that language may be understood as a computational system of symbols that is ultimately realized in the neural structure of the brain, and that the logical structures of thought mirror the causal relations of neural processes (Jerry A. Fodor, *Psychosemantics: The Problem of Meaning in the Philosophy of Mind* [Cambridge, MA: Bradford Books/MIT Press, 1987]).

5. Eliminative materialism is the view that talk of selves and subjective qualitative states in general can, in principle, be replaced by third-person accounts of brain states and biological processes. This position does not deny that concepts of the self relate to genuine features of human beings. What it argues is that human behavior will, in the future, be more accurately described, explained, and predicted by neuroscientific accounts rather than by first-person or phenomenological accounts.

6. For Dennett:

I . . . like Churchland's alternative idea of propositional attitude statements as indirect "measurements" of a reality diffused in the behavioral dispositions of the brain (and body). We think beliefs are quite real enough to call real just so long as belief-talk measures these complex behavior-disposing organs as predictively as it does (Dennett, *Brainchildren*, pp. 113–14).

See also Paul M. Churchland, *Scientific Realism and the Plasticity of Mind* (Cambridge: Cambridge University Press, 1979) and *A Neurocomputational Perspective: The Nature of Mind and the Structure of Science* (Cambridge, MA: MIT Press, 1990).

7. Dennett, *Brainchildren*, p. 119. See also a similar dis-

cussion in *The Intentional Stance,* where Dennett claims that physical descriptions of human events (carried out by highly intelligent Martians) will inevitably be more complicated than the intentional language of human beings (pp. 22–27).

8. Daniel Dennett, "Back from the Drawing Board," in *Dennett and His Critics,* ed. Bo Dahlbom (Oxford: Blackwell, 1993), p. 234.

9. Daniel Dennett, *Consciousness Explained (CE)* (London: Penguin, 1991), pp. 70–98. Briefly, heterophenomenology is Dennett's attempt to combine Husserlian phenomenology with his brand of naturalism. Dennett acknowledges that he based his heterophenomenological method on Husserl's phenomenology, albeit at a distance, as he had not read Husserl since he studied him as an undergraduate. See Dennett, *Consciousness Explained,* p. 44 and "With a Little Help from My Friends," in *Dennett's Philosophy, A Comprehensive Assessment,* ed. Don Ross, Andrew Brook, and David Thompson (Cambridge, MA: MIT Press, 2000), p. 362.

10. See Dennett, "With a Little Help from My Friends," pp. 327–88 and Dennett, "The Fantasy of First-Person Science," *Third Draft,* March 1, http://ase.tufts.edu/cogstud/papers/chalmersdeb3dft.htm (accessed August 14, 2006).

11. In *CE,* the HM focused solely on the analysis of first-person reports; however, in response to critics of heterophenomenology Dennett has more recently acknowledged that the HM is also concerned with physiological data. See ibid., "The Fantasy of First-Person Science," p. 2.

12. Dennett, *CE,* p. 83.

13. Ibid., p. 44. Briefly, Husserl argues that judgments based on common sense or scientific and philosophical frameworks about the mind-independent existence of objects have to be suspended or bracketed (epoché). Instead, the phenomenologist's task involves a full description of what is presented to

conscious experience in everyday life. In one essay, Dennett acknowledges that the neutrality of the heterophenomenologist is the same as that created by the bracketing of the epoché: "We [Husserl and Dennett] are kindred spirits, and the epoché is our point of closest agreement, from either side of our first-person/third-person starting points" (Dennett, "With a Little Help from My Friends," p. 363).

14. Dennett, *The Intentional Stance*, p. 17.

15. Dennett, "With a Little Help from My Friends," pp. 362–63.

16. Dennett, *CE*, p. 94.

17. Dennett, "The Fantasy of First-Person Science," p. 2.

18. Dennett, *CE*, p. 84.

19. Ibid., p. 85.

20. Ibid., pp. 101–102.

21. Ibid., p. 33. For more recent defenses of Cartesian dualism, see John Foster, *The Immaterial Self* (London: Routledge, 1991) and David J. Chalmers, *The Conscious Mind: In Search of a Fundamental Theory* (Oxford: Oxford University Press, 1996).

22. Descartes suggests that the location of interaction between mind and body is the pineal gland (described by Dennett as "the turnstile of consciousness" in *CE*, p. 105). It is important to point out that Dennett reads Descartes as the inspiration for, rather than the originator of, accounts of the self that he describes as "real." Dennett draws the latter in far cruder terms than Descartes himself might have been happy with. For a more sympathetic reading of Descartes' account of the relationship between mind and body, see Annette Baier's chapter, "Cartesian Persons," in her book, *Postures of the Mind* (Minneapolis: University of Minnesota Press, 1985), pp. 74–92. See also Bernard William's entry on Descartes in *The Concise Encyclopaedia of Western Philosophy and Philosophers*, ed.

J. O. Urmson and Jonathan Rée (London: Unwin Hyman, 1989), pp. 72–78.

23. Gilbert Ryle, *The Concept of Mind* (London: Hutchinson, 1949).

24. Dennett, *CE*, p. 107.

25. Dennett acknowledges that few contemporary theorists would explicitly endorse Cartesian materialism. Presumably, this is in light of the fact that neuroscientific research has all but excluded the possibility of any direct referent for the self in the brain/body. However, the point that Dennett is making is that the central ideas behind Cartesian materialism/dualism continue to inspire contemporary accounts of consciousness, albeit implicitly.

26. Daniel Dennett, "Get Real," *Philosophical Topics* 22, nos. 1 and 2 (1994): 540.

27. Dennett, *CE*, pp. 356–62, 323–24. John Locke was among the first to focus attention on the idea of consciousness as continuous and the implications thereof. This idea was subsequently taken up by William James, who describes consciousness as streamlike:

Consciousness, then, does not appear to itself chopped up in bits. Such words as "chain" or "train" do not describe it fitly as it presents itself in the first instance. It is nothing jointed; it flows. A "river" or a "stream" are the metaphors by which it is most naturally described. In talking of it hereafter, let us call it the stream of thought, of consciousness, or of subjective life (William James, "The Stream of Consciousness," in *Modern Philosophy of Mind*, ed. William Lyons [London: Everyman, 1995]. Originally published in 1892).

28. Dennett, *CE*, pp. 120–28. The color phi phenomenon refers to an experiment where a red flash occurs on the left of the visual field, followed by a green flash on the right of the field. In this scenario, what the subject reports is a single spot moving and changing midtrajectory from red to green. The Cartesian model with its depiction of consciousness as stream-like cannot explain why the subject fails to see the initial stationary flash.

29. Dennett, *CE*, pp. 257–58. The binding problem refers to the way in which the brain somehow unifies disparate perceptions such as the smell, taste, color, and texture of ice cream, given that the senses (hearing, smelling, tasting, seeing, and touching) are based in different areas of the cortex and paleocortex. The Cartesian model accounts for the unity of perceptions by locating them in some central place. However, granted that there is no empirical evidence for such a place, the Cartesian model fails to explain how these different perceptions are unified.

30. Dennett, *CE*, pp. 322–33. Blindsight refers to visual perception without apparent awareness. This is the ability of people with a blind spot in their visual field (caused by damage to a portion of the occipital cortex on the opposite side of the blind spot) to nevertheless accurately "guess" that a light or particular shape has been flashed in their blind field. As with his other examples, Dennett's argument here is that the Cartesian theory of consciousness cannot account for the phenomenon of blindsight.

31. I don't claim to offer a full explanation of Dennett's alternatives to Cartesian materialism, which have been the source of a great deal of debate since 1991. For example, he deploys other interesting metaphors to describe mental activity, such as the Joycean machine (*CE*, ch. 9). The latter combines his computational account of mental activity

(MDM) with an emphasis on human linguistic ability and an evolutionary explanation of the origins of consciousness. For a thorough empirically oriented exegesis of the MDM see Kathleen Akins, "Lost the Plot? Reconstructing Dennett's Multiple Drafts Theory of Consciousness," *Mind and Language* 11, no. 1 (1996): 1–43. For analyses that focus more on the philosophical problems that the MDM raises, see Robert Kirk, "'The Best Set of Tools?' Dennett's Metaphors and the Mind-Body Problem," *Philosophical Quarterly* 43, no. 172 (1993): 334–43 and Ned Block, "What is Dennett's Theory a Theory Of?" *Philosophical Topics* 22, nos. 1 and 2 (1994): 23–40.

32. Dennett, *CE*, pp. 253–54.

33. Ibid., p. 136.

34. Ibid., pp. 136, 253–54.

35. Dennett, "Get Real," p. 531.

36. Dennett, *CE*, p. 24. Consciousness is described in the following way: "Although like love, [consciousness] has an elaborate biological base, like money, some of its most significant features are borne along on the culture, not simply inherent, somehow in the physical structure of its instances" (p. 24).

37. Daniel Dennett, "The Message Is: There Is No Medium," *Philosophy and Phenomenological Research* 53 no. 4 (1993): 928–29.

38. See Daniel Dennett, "Real Consciousness," in *Consciousness in Philosophy and Cognitive Science*, ed. A. Revonsuo and M. Kamppinen (Hillsdale, NJ: Lawrence Erlbaum, 1994), pp. 55–63 and "Are We Explaining Consciousness Yet?" *Cognition* 79 nos. 1–2 (2001): 221–37.

39. Dennett, "The Message is: There is no Medium."

40. David J. Chalmers claims that there is an explanatory gap between the "easy" (e.g., discrimination, conscious control, reportability) and the "hard" (i.e., experience) problems of

consciousness. See Chalmers, *The Conscious Mind: In Search of a Fundamental Theory* (Oxford: Oxford University Press, 1996).

    41. Thomas Nagel expresses the problem as the fact that there is "something it is like" to be a conscious organism (see Nagel, *A View from Nowhere* [Oxford: Oxford University Press, 1974] and "What Is It Like to Be a Bat?" *Philosophical Review* 4 [1986]: 435-50). John Searle suggests that Dennett has simply explained consciousness away (see Searle, *The Rediscovery of the Mind* [Cambridge, MA: MIT Press, 1992] and "Consciousness Denied: Daniel Dennett's Account," in *The Mystery of Consciousness* [London: Granta Publications, 1998], pp. 98-131). Margaret Boden mischievously advises that she regards Dennett's title of his 1991 book, *Consciousness Explained*, as "inviting prosecution under the Trade Descriptions Act." (see Boden, "Consciousness and Human Identity: An Interdisciplinary Perspective," in *Consciousness and Human Identity*, ed. John Cornwell [Oxford: Oxford University Press, 1998], p. 10).

Chapter Two

THE NATURALIST NARRATIVE SELF

Since 1983, Dennett has argued that the views of the self that he descriptively terms "self as a soul-pearl" or "Cartesian Theater" should be replaced by a notion of the self as a "center of narrative gravity":[1]

> A self, according to my theory, is not any old mathe-matical point, but an abstraction defined by the myriads of attributions and interpretations (including self attributions and self- interpretations) that have composed the biography of the living body whose Center of Narrative Gravity it is.[2]

In describing the self as a "center of narrative gravity," Dennett indicates that it is not real in the way that a "living body" is real. Rather, he sees it as a unity that is constructed out of the many ways in which that life and body can be narrated and described, including the way that life and body are interpreted from a personal point of view. In short, in line with the heterophenomenological method (HM) outlined in chapter 1, Dennett's claim is that first- and third-person accounts of experience and behavior contribute to the constitution of selfhood. There are two concepts to be unpacked here: a center of gravity and narrative. What emerges from Dennett's delineation of both of these concepts combined with his multiple draft model of consciousness (MDM), also outlined in chapter 1, is a model of the narrative self.

In Newtonian physics, Dennett understands that items such as centers of gravity are postulated as "abstractions"—"theorist's fictions" that are, nevertheless, part of a rational explanation of the behavior of physical objects.[3] By this, he means that they are causal explanations of a sort, in the sense that they can, for instance, account for why physical items might teeter or fall.[4] From this, he concludes that "centers of gravity are real because they are (somehow) good abstract objects. They deserve to be taken seriously, learned about, used."[5] Dennett is careful, however, to distinguish the ontological status of centers of gravity described as *abstracta* from other theoretical entities described as *illata*.[6] The latter are entities that refer to a mind-independent reality that is theoretically inferred, that is, they are concrete things. On the contrary, *abstracta* are theoretical items whose properties are constituted wholly by the theory within which they are deployed. They do *not* refer to any underlying physical data, and so, for example, the center of gravity has no shape or color:

> But a center of gravity is not an atom or a subatomic particle or any other physical item in the world. It has

no mass; it has no color. . . . It is, if you like, a theorist's
fiction. It is not one of the real things in the universe
in addition to the atoms. But it is a fiction that has a
nicely defined, well-delineated and well-behaved role
within physics.[7]

Granted, then, that centers of gravity are useful fictions
for the purposes of better understanding the behavior of
physical objects, it follows that the concept of self,
defined as a center of gravity, is an abstraction that can be
evaluated not on the basis of its ontological status, but on
the basis of its explanatory power.

Dennett describes the center of gravity as a "narrative
gravity" in light of his commitment to the basic tenets of
evolutionary biology which, he argues, explain the cognitive capacities and behavior of human beings and
account for the fact that we "spin" ourselves.[8] What he
sees as unique to human beings is the ability to self-rep-
resent in language. While biological systems minimally
organize boundaries in terms of shells, skin, or teams
(lobsters, tigers, or termites), humans significantly
organize boundaries narratively.[9] "Our fundamental
tactic of self-protection, self-control, and self-definition is
not spinning webs or building dams, but telling stories,
and more particularly concocting the story we tell
others—and ourselves—about who we are."[10] Accepting
that humans have the capacity to tell stories about themselves, he construes the narrative as an organizing principle and a way in which human beings define boundaries between themselves and others.

And just as spiders don't have to think, consciously and deliberatively, about how to spin their webs, and just as beavers, unlike professional human engineers, do not consciously and deliberately plan the structures they build, we (unlike professional human storytellers) do not consciously and deliberatively figure out what narratives to tell and how to tell them. Our tales are spun, but for the most part we don't spin them; they spin us. Our human consciousness, and our narrative selfhood, is their product, not their source. These strings or streams of narrative issue forth *as if* from a single source—not just in the obvious physical sense of flowing from just one mouth, or one pencil or pen, but in a more subtle sense: their effect on any audience or readers is to encourage them to (try to) posit a unified agent whose words they are, about whom they are: in short, to posit what I call a *center of narrative gravity*.[11]

Dennett envisages an apparently purposeful and integrated decision maker that is *in fact* a collection of conscious and nonconscious specialized subsystems and communication networks, the MDM. The point here is that, at the source, there are only "strings or streams of narrative" that are interpreted "as if" they come from a single self in the course of interaction with an audience or readers. In sum, he claims the idea that there is a unified consciousness—or a single self who speaks, writes, or acts—is the outcome of processes that are largely unconscious and nondeliberative, just as the web and the dam are the outcome of unconscious and nondeliberative activities of spiders and beavers.

By describing the self as a center of narrative gravity, Dennett holds on to the concept of the self as theoretically useful while at the same time uncoupling it from the idea that it is real in the sense of being a distinct entity or object located in the brain. Ignoring the sense of narrative as factual (such as history and biography), he describes narrative unity as a "fictive self" in order to emphasize its nonreal status:[12]

> We might say indeed that the self is rather like the "center of narrative gravity" of a set of biographical events and tendencies; but, as with a center of physical gravity, there's really no such *thing* (with mass or shape). Let's call this nonrealist picture of the self, the idea of a "fictive-self."[13]

The notion of self as fictive is opposed to the notion of the self as "proper" or "real":

> Ask a layman what he thinks a self is, and his unreflecting answer will probably be that a person's self is indeed some kind of real thing: a ghostly supervisor who lives inside his head, the thinker of his thoughts, the repository of his memories, the holder of his values, his conscious inner "I." Although he might be unlikely these days to use the term "soul," it would be very much the age-old conception of the soul that he would have in mind. A self (or soul) is an existent entity with executive powers over the body and its own enduring qualities. Let's call this realist picture of the self, the idea of a "proper self."[14]

PUZZLE CASES

Dennett makes positive use of puzzle cases in order to draw out the differences and, also, the similarities between his fictive self and the Cartesian proper self. The particular cases he selects—multiple personality, immortality, and split-brain (explained below)—muddy the waters for the Cartesian view and support the narrative view, because they are not simply pathological exceptions to the norm; rather, for Dennett, they are examples of the normal fragmentation of human experience and behavior. Moreover, even as Dennett draws attention to the differences between both Cartesian and narrative accounts, he also indicates significant similarities—in short, both theories deploy *similar concepts* of the self, however different their ontological reference might be. This is in keeping with Dennett's general naturalist strategy that seeks to retain psychological language as an explanatory tool. Dennett's aim is twofold: On the one hand, he seeks to disengage the language of the self from bogus dualisms; on the other hand, he seeks to prevent its dissipation and replacement by the language of the neurosciences. The tensions between Dennett's narrative model of the self and the Cartesian alternative are more clearly understood through an examination of Dennett's treatment of the three familiar puzzle cases that follow.

Multiple personality

On Dennett's account, Multiple Personality is neither a scientific nor a logical impossibility. He claims that, for some people, it may be the only way of coping with their life's experiences.[15] Assuming that a human being is born as an individual organism while self-like features emerge as the organism interacts with the world, he draws the implication that "two or three or seventeen selves per body is really no more metaphysically extravagant than one self per body."[16] Dennett conceives the mind "as a coalition or bundle of semi-independent agencies" and differentiates selves as "quasi-selves, semi-selves, transitional selves."[17] This differentiation is not necessarily based on the physical location of these selves. It is not self-evident that there should exist one self per body; selves are not "brain-pearls"; they are not strictly countable or locatable in the way that the brain might be.[18] There may be more than one self, as with those who have a Multiple Personality Disorder (MPD) (a number of selves to a body), or there may be less than one self as with those who have a Fractional Personality Disorder (one self to more than one body).[19] In support of the latter, Dennett cites the case of identical twins, Greta and Freda Chaplin, who seemed in speech and behavior to "act as one."[20]

Applied to any given therapeutic situation involving a person with MPD, it follows that even though there may be grounds for positing the achievement of a single self as the goal of a particular therapy, that goal is neither inevitable nor necessarily desirable. The important point for Dennett, which is outlined in an article he coauthors with Nicholas Humphrey, "Speaking for Our Selves," is that arguments in support of such a goal would have to be made:

They [alters] are what they are—they are selves, for
want of a better word. As selves, they are as real as
any self could be; they are not imaginary playmates or
theatrical roles on the one hand, nor on the other
hand are they ghostly people or eternal souls sharing
a mortal body. It is possible for some therapists, apparently, to tiptoe between these extremes, respecting
without *endorsing* the alters, sustaining enough trust
and peace of mind in their patients to continue
therapy effectively while eschewing the equally (or
even more) effective therapeutic route of frank
endorsement (with its attendant exaggerations) followed by "fusion" or "integration." Anyone who finds
this middle road hard to imagine should *try harder to
imagine it* before declaring it a conceptual impossibility.[21]

However, the puzzle case of MPD overall reveals that
this account of the self is close to the Cartesian account
in significant ways. In the case of MPD, at least some of
the personalities are genuinely separate selves because,
for Humphrey and Dennett, "the grounds for assigning
several selves to such a human being *can be as good
as—indeed the same as—those for assigning a single
self to a normal human being.*"[22] They argue that a
number of conditions need to be met in order that a case
of MPD be real. These conditions can be summarized as
follows:

- The subject (individual with MPD) will have different "spokesmen," "Heads of Mind" corresponding to different selves because the spokesmen

will have access to different sets of memories, attitudes and thoughts.

- Each self, when present, will claim to have conscious control over the subject's behavior and ownership of her thoughts, experiences, memories, actions. Each self, when "out front," may be conscious of the existence *of* other selves, but she will not be conscious *with* them.
- Each self will be convinced by "her own rhetoric" about her own integrity and personal importance.
- This self-rhetoric will be convincing to the subject but also to others with whom the subject interacts.
- Different selves will present themselves in interestingly different ways, e.g., phlegmatic, out of control, or carnal. Each style of presentation will likely be associated with differences in physiology.
- The "splitting" into separate selves will likely predate the therapeutic situation.[23]

Extrapolating from these criteria, a single self involves a single narrator with access to one set of memories, attitudes, and thoughts; who claims to have conscious control over her behavior and ownership of her experiences; who cares for her own well-being; whose self representations are accepted by herself and others; and who presents herself to others with an individual emotional style that may be related to underlying physiological dispositions.

From this extrapolation, it is clear that on the Dennettian account of the self, whether there be multiple selves or fragmented selves, the explanation of human behavior requires the postulation of some kind of self who plays a causal role in the behavior of the individual. Moreover, moral features are also included—self-importance and integrity—as a condition of being a single self. This inclusion is important, because along with linguistic ability, these features pull Dennett's position further away from the minimal kind of selfhood that humans share with animals, or many multiples display, toward an account of a higher-order kind of self that is distinctively human.

It is also clear that Dennett is not entirely disinterested in the number of selves that may be assigned to a single individual, nor is he disinterested in the kind of features that such a self might display. For example, in "The Origin of Selves," Dennett cites neurophysiological evidence indicating that the brain prefers coherence and single-mindedness to dissonance and conflict.[24] Humphrey and Dennett also argue that human beings may function better from a social and psychological point of view with one "Head of Mind." This is because "language-producing systems of the brain have to get their instructions from somewhere" (though they note that this only ensures the unity of "clusters of speech," not the unity of a single author over time).[25] For most people one version of "the real me" is favored, and that is installed as the "Head of Mind."[26] The self as the "Head of Mind" is posited at a level in between the idea of a "proper-self"—"a ghostly supervisor who lives inside his head, the thinker of his thoughts, the repository of his memories, the holder of his values, his conscious inner

'I'"—and an entirely arbitrary fictive self.[27] So, while all selves are narrated, one self emerges to play a role in the life of the human being in much the same way as a president might play the role of figurehead of a country: "In short, a human being too may need an inner figurehead—especially given the complexities of human social life ... with a real, if limited, causal role to play in representing the person to himself and to the world."[28] Dennett also makes an important distinction between "fragmentary selves," such as those of the MPD patient, and "fully fledged selves," such as those of most other people who have the right "sort" of autobiography.[29] He points out that in the case of most MPD patients there "simply aren't enough waking hours in the day" for them to "accrue the sort of autobiography of which fully fledged selves are made."[30]

Adding these claims—that the human being functions better as a single self and that such a self ought to be "fully fledged"—to the extrapolated model drawn from MPD and what Dennett is describing are the core features of selves that any Cartesian-inspired theory of proper or real selves would include. Even granting that there is no empirical evidence of a locatable, single self (in the brain or elsewhere), the postulation of a self—whether single, multiple, or fragmented—remains a compelling element of his explanation of human behavior. What his account of multiple personality demonstrates, then, is that there may be more or less than one self, *not* that there is no longer any explanatory need to postulate the notion of *some kind* of self.

Immortality

While the phenomenon of multiple personality raises problems regarding the unity of the self at any one time, the question of survival after death raises the problem of its continuity over time. In one passage, cited below, Dennett claims that his model of the narrative self can deliver what Cartesian-inspired accounts cannot—survival of the self after the death of the body. If the self were a soul substance of some kind, then, according to Dennett, its immortality can only be explained on the grounds that there is some kind of peculiar "soul-stuff" with immortal properties (which is theoretically strange and practically unlikely).[31] In addition, if the self were a material substance, a particular set of brain atoms, then its immortality would rest on the possibility of these atoms remaining together after the rest of the body perished (which also seems unlikely). However, as a center of narrative gravity, the immortality of the self is more likely and more conceivable:

> If you think of yourself as a center of narrative gravity, on the other hand, your existence depends on the persistence of that narrative (rather like the Thousand and One Arabian Nights, but all a single tale), which could *theoretically* survive indefinitely many switches of *medium*, be teleported as readily (in principle) as the evening news, and stored indefinitely as sheer information. If what you are is that organization of information that has structured your body's control system (or, to put it in its more usual provocative form, if what you are is the program that runs on your brain's com-

puter), then you could in principle survive the death of your body as intact as a program can survive the destruction of the computer on which it was created and first run.[32]

The description of the narrative self as the computer software program running on the hardware computer of the brain certainly allows that such a self can survive many physical manifestations. In addition, descriptions that deploy computational language may be more appealing to contemporary readers than the language of souls.

However, there are problems with this puzzle case. To put it bluntly, it strikes me that the construal of the self as an "organization of information," distinguished in such a radical way from the human body and from existence in time, is profoundly counterintuitive. In which case the fact that Dennett's account delivers immortality and the others don't is not a convincing argument in its favor. This is because the immortality offered is so distant from that traditionally argued for, that the gesture toward a promise of immortality is empty.[33] Worrying about the immortality of such a self would be similar to worrying about the immortality of a first edition; perhaps even less so. Dennett has so altered the meaning of the concept of the self and the concept of immortality in this theory that they no longer relate to any familiar notions of the self nor display any of the features which theories of the self attempt to explain, for example, the sense of ownership of one's body.

Dennett might well argue that this is not an issue for

him, since on his view it is the layperson's intuitions about the proper self that he is challenging. However, I do think that it is an issue for him, because the problem of immortality and any solutions to it pertain to a more robust notion of the self than his definition of it allows. Even the supposedly misguided layperson is unlikely to be persuaded by the Dennettian account of immortality. Consider the process of grief and bereavement. Does the promise that our loved ones can be immortalized if they are stored as "sheer information" on a computer software program alleviate any of the pain we suffer at their loss? Dennett's theory of the narrative self cannot justifiably gain support from finding a solution to a problem that his conceptualization of the self does not genuinely have—who cares if "sheer information" is immortal or not?

Alternatively, the immortality of, for example, the Lockean self is a very important matter. Locke's account of personal identity in chapter 27 of *Essay concerning Human Understanding* posits the self as a unity that is constituted by consciousness.[34] For Locke, the self emerges with conscious thought and its underlying nature as soul or body is allegedly irrelevant to the determinations of its identity and function. His thesis on personal identity is primarily intended to provide an account of the self as someone who is concerned about her future, capable of immortality, morally responsible, and accountable. The Lockean formulation of the problem of personal identity could be viewed as anticipating contemporary interest in conceiving the self narratively because of its mixed metaphysical underpinnings, its focus on delivering a particular kind of self, and its attention to the self-constituting aspects of consciousness. However, on Locke's account, whether or not the self was construed as immortal had important implications for the behavior of the mortal self. In short, the promise of immortality entered into human decision making because it meant that human actions would be judged and rewarded or punished in the afterlife. Alternatively, the Dennettian "center of narrative gravity" defined as an "organization of information" delivers immortality at the price of denuding the self of the very characteristics that make it something one might be interested in preserving.[35]

Split-Brain

Since A. L. Wigan's classic text *A New View of Insanity: The Duality of the Mind* in 1844, and later the award of the Nobel Prize in physiology to Roger Sperry acknowledging his work with split-brain subjects in 1981, there has been debate in the natural and human sciences as to whether or not each human being has a single consciousness.[36] Given the Cartesian assumption that consciousness is the ground of experiences of selfhood, whether or not consciousness is unified (or fragmented in Dennett's case) has important implications for any theory about the unity of selves. The fact that people, whose hemispheres have been surgically divided, sometimes behave as if they have two mutually disinterested and conflicting seats of consciousness gives support to the claim that consciousness resides independently in each hemisphere.[37] Addressing the American Psychological Association in Washington, DC, in 1967, Sperry concluded that, in what he called the minor hemisphere,

> [W]e deal with a second conscious entity that is characteristically human and runs along in parallel with the more dominant stream of consciousness in the major hemisphere. . . . There is no indication that the dominant mental system of the left hemisphere is concerned about or even aware of the presence of the minor system under most ordinary conditions except quite indirectly as, for example, through occasional responses triggered from the minor side. As one patient remarked immediately after seeing herself make a left-hand response of this kind, "Now I know it wasn't me did that!"[38]

Does it then follow that split-brain patients have two selves? Dennett strongly rejects the idea that brain bifurcation has any bearing on the counting of selves. He insists that the self is not concrete, locatable, or countable in the way a physical entity like the brain is, so that even if there were one, two, three, or four brains, it does not follow that there has to be one or more selves.[39] If Dennett denies *one* self is concrete, locatable, or countable, then, a fortiori, two selves are not locatable or countable. In the case of bifurcation, Dennett acknowledges that a temporary "second center of gravity" may thereby be created. However, the problem with such a second center is that it is not sufficiently enduring to accrue the kind of autobiography necessary for a "fully fledged self."[40] Moreover, he associates "narrative richness" with the capacities of the left hemisphere of the brain and claims that the conditions for accumulating the level of narrative richness that would be sufficient to constitute a "fully fledged" self are not present in the right hemisphere self of a split-brain patient.[41] He imagines what for him would be the frustrating and chilling prospect of being a right-hemisphere self in a split-brain patient, and his horror rests in the inability of the right-hemisphere to verbalize, though clearly it still communicates.

> You would like to tell the world what it is like to be you, but you can't! You're cut off from all verbal communication by the loss of your indirect phone lines to the radio station in the left hemisphere. You do your best to signal your existence to the outside world, tugging your half of the face into lopsided frowns and smiles, and occasionally (if you are a virtuoso right hemisphere self) scrawling a word or two with your left hand.[42]

What emerges from his treatment of the split-brain puzzle case is the thesis that narrative ability is a condition for the possibility of a higher-order or fully fledged self and that, in human beings, this condition is met, as a matter of fact, by neural processes in the left hemisphere of the brain. The point that Dennett is anxious to make is that in positing such a condition he is not privileging any particular kind of medium for its realization. This means that in the human case, the medium is certain processes in the left hemisphere; in other possible cases, the medium might be micro chips or green goo.[43] In the case of brain bifurcation then, only one of the two con-

sciousnesses, resulting from brain bifurcation, is relevant
to the number of selves that can be counted. Because this
is a similar situation to the one that pertained prior to the
split, Dennett can conclude that brain bifurcation is irrelevant to the counting of selves.

What Dennett leaves undisturbed in his account of
brain bifurcation is the requirement of narrative richness
for the possibility of there being a fully fledged self. While
it is unclear what he wants to include in the term "narrative richness," minimally it requires linguistic ability of a
kind that enables a human being to communicate an
intelligible account of her behavior to others. Thus,
even as Dennett distinguishes his account from traditional views by arguing that the self is narrated, his claim
that even a narrative self must have linguistic ability
places his theory of the self firmly in a philosophical tradition, shared by Descartes and Locke and reaching back
to Aristotle and Boethius. They take the linguistic ability
of human beings as a condition of features like rationality, intelligence, and accountability and take these features in turn to mark a significant distinction between
humans and animals.

In sum, Dennett's deployment of these puzzle
cases—multiple personality, immortality, and split-
brain—as a means of teasing out the similarities and differences between his account of the narrative self and
the Cartesian alternative shows that, for Dennett:

- one or more selves may emerge per human body,
  but usually one emerges if it meets a certain
  number of conditions;

- the narrative self, understood as a computer program or organization of information (rather than as spirit or matter), is, in some sense, immortal;
- the self is not tied to a particular kind of medium (spirit or matter), but rather it is conditional on linguistic ability.

As already indicated, these puzzle cases are not unproblematic and, in particular, I will discuss Dennett's requirement of linguistic ability as a condition of narrative selfhood in more detail in chapter 3.

THE HETEROPHENOMENOLOGICAL METHOD AND THE NARRATIVE SELF

To recap, Dennett wants to retain a role for psychological language, including self-talk, in any explanation of human life. His strategy is to employ naturalist models of explanation such as the HM to achieve this. Recall that Dennett posits the HM as an alternative to other naturalist solutions to the problem of relating the mental and physical, the mind and brain. While Dennett does not explicitly apply the HM to the problem of the self, it is possible to do so if we combine his accounts of the Multiple Drafts Model of consciousness and the self as a center of gravity along with his evolutionary explanation of narrativity. What emerges is an illustration of the HM and its four different elements at work. As indicated in chapter 1 in relation to the phenomenon of consciousness, the application of the HM involved: gathering the data of first-person reports of conscious experience, observing subjects' emotional and physiological behavior, bracketing any worries about the ontological status of the objects of conscious experience, and taking a third-person stance toward the phenomena concerned. In general, then, the HM is concerned with first-person or subjective reports of experience, objective descriptions of publicly available or observable phenomena, the bracketing of ontological questions, and the assumption of third-person stances.

Applied to the phenomenon of the self, what emerges is the following: First, the narrative self is cast as a unity based on life stories (autobiographical and biographical accounts). Second, the narrative self is cast as referring to the (supposedly more) scientifically robust account of brain processes, the MDM of consciousness. Third, ontological questions are bracketed: the concept of the narrative self is considered to be theoretically useful even though it is not considered real (scientifically determinable). Fourth, the narrative self is viewed as the product of evolutionary design and as theoretically useful because it is possible to better predict human behavior by treating human beings as purposeful and integrated decision makers (the intentional stance). In sum, Dennett's model of the narrative self fulfills each of the tasks that are central features of the HM and shows that Dennett, albeit implicitly, is consistent in applying the naturalist strategy that he has developed. Granted the innovativeness of Dennett's approach, several objections can be leveled at his account of the narrative self, which I explore in the following chapter.

NOTES TO CHAPTER 2

1. Dennett, *CE*, pp. 427, 431. As early as 1979, Dennett anticipated his account of the self as a "theorist's fiction" in his essay on the "Conditions of Personhood" where he concluded that:

> [i]t might turn out, for instance, that the concept of a person is only a free-floating honorific that we are all happy to apply to ourselves, and to others as the spirit moves us, guided by our emotions, aesthetic sensibilities, considerations of policy, and the like—just as those who are *chic* are all and only those who can get themselves considered *chic* by others who consider themselves *chic*. (Daniel Dennett, *Brainstorms* [Sussex: Harvester Press, 1979], p. 268)

Dennett also gave a lecture on the "Self as the Center of Narrative Gravity" in Houston in 1983.

An abridged version was subsequently published in the *Times Literary Supplement* as "Why Everyone Is a Novelist," *Times Literary Supplement* 4, no. 459 (1988): 1016-29. Similar and more detailed versions have appeared in *Cogito* (Daniel Dennett, "The Origin of Selves," *Cogito* 21 [1989]: 163-73). See also Nicholas Humphrey and Daniel Dennett, "Speaking for Our Selves," *Brainchildren* by Daniel Dennett (London: Penguin, 1998), pp. 31-55. Originally published in *Raritan: A Quarterly Review* 9 (Summer 1989): 68-98.

2. Dennett, *CE*, pp. 426-27.

3. Ibid., p. 429. Dennett starts chapter 5 of *CE* with an interesting quotation from William James, who claims there is no material evidence for the existence of a "keystone" or "center of gravity" in the brain. Perhaps it is this reference of

James that prompted Dennett to amplify the latter notion in support of his own thesis. James had written: "There is no cell or group of cells in the brain of such anatomical or functional preeminece as to appear to be the keystone or center of gravity of the whole system" (cited in Dennett, *CE*, p. 101).

4. A causal explanation of a jug falling to the floor is: "Jim pushed it off the shelf," or, put another way: "Its center of gravity shifted."

5. Dennett, *Brainchildren*, p. 97.

6. Dennett, "Why Everyone Is a Novelist," p. 1016. The distinction between *abstracta* and *illata* was first made by Hans Reichenbach (1891–1953), who was closely associated with the Logical Positivist movement and is the author of *The Rise of Scientific Philosophy* (Berkeley: University of California Press, 1951). As far as I know, Dennett first made use of the distinction in *The Intentional Stance*.

7. Dennett, "Why Everyone Is a Novelist," p. 1016.

8. Dennett, "The Origin of Selves," p. 169; Dennett, *CE*, p. 418.

9. Dennett defines the biological self as the ability to distinguish between self and other, which, in the case of natural organisms generally, is porous and indefinite (e.g., bodies have shells, webs, or interloping bacteria within). And, for Dennett, human beings evolve the most complex of selves:

> But the strangest and most wonderful constructions in the whole animal world are the amazing, intricate constructions made by the primate, *Homo sapiens*. Each normal individual of this species makes a self. Out of its brain it spins a web of words and deeds, and, like the other creatures, it doesn't have to know what it's doing: it just does it. This web protects it, just like the snail's shell, and provides it a livelihood, just like the

spider's web, and advances its prospects for sex, just like the bowerbird's bower (Dennett, *CE*, p. 416).

10. Ibid., p. 418.

11. Dennett, "The Origin of Selves," p. 169.

12. Ignoring the fact that a "narrative" may be concerned with both factual as well as fictional events is an oversight that limits the way in which Dennett may construe the narrative self. This limitation is further examined in chapter 3.

13. Humphrey and Dennett, "Speaking for Our Selves," pp. 38-39. Elsewhere, Dennett describes the self as "fictional" in the following terms:

That is, it does seem that we are all virtuoso novelists, who find ourselves engaged in all sorts of behavior, more or less unified, but sometimes disunified, and we always put the best "faces" on if we can. We try to make all of our material cohere into a single good story. And that story is our autobiography. The chief fictional character at the center of that autobiography is one's self (Dennett, "Why Everyone Is a Novelist," p. 1029).

14. Humphrey and Dennett, "Speaking for Our Selves," p. 38.

15. Ibid., p. 54.

16. Dennett, *CE*, p. 419.

17. Ibid., pp. 260, 424-25.

18. Ibid., p. 424.

19. Multiple Personality Disorder is now called Dissociative Identity Disorder by the American Psychiatric Association (APA). While the APA increasingly acknowledges controversies surrounding the diagnosis and distinctiveness of Dissociative

Identity Disorder, one criterion for the presence of the disorder is significant: "the presence of two or more distinct identities or personality states . . . that recurrently take control of behavior" (American Psychiatric Association, *Diagnostic and Statistical Manual of Mental Disorders*, 4th ed. [Washington, DC: American Psychiatric Association, 1994], p. 484).

20. Dennett, *CE*, p. 422; Dennett, "The Origin of Selves," p. 165.

21. Humphrey and Dennett, "Speaking for Our Selves," pp. 57-58.

22. Ibid., p. 54

23. Ibid., p. 45. This is a brief sketch of the conditions set by Humphrey and Dennett. See the text for the complete account.

24. Dennett, "The Origin of Selves," p. 173.

25. Humphrey and Dennett, "Speaking for Our Selves," p. 43.

26. Ibid., p. 42.

27. Ibid., pp. 38-39.

28. Ibid., p. 41.

29. Dennett, *CE*, p. 425.

30. Ibid.

31. Ibid., p. 430.

32. Ibid.

33. The same could be said of Dennett's more recent argument for a "mimetic" self where memes, like genes, don't depend on individual organisms for their realization. See Daniel Dennett, *Darwin's Dangerous Idea* (London: Penguin, 1995).

34. John Locke, *An Essay Concerning Human Understanding*, ed. Peter H. Nidditch (Oxford: Clarendon, 1975). Originally published in 1694.

35. Dennett, *CE*, p. 430.

36. Arthur Ladbroke Wigan, *A New View of Insanity: The Duality of the Mind* (London: Longmans, 1844).

37. The brain is not literally halved: rather, the network of nerves, called the corpus callossum, that links both hemispheres is cut, thereby severing direct communication between them.

38. R.W. Sperry, "Hemisphere Deconnection and Unity in Conscious Awareness," in *Self and Identity: Contemporary Philosophical Issues*, ed. Daniel Kolak and Raymond Martin (New York: Macmillan, 1991), p. 67.

39. Dennett, *CE*, p. 424

40. Ibid., p. 425.

41. Ibid., p. 426.

42. Ibid.

43. Ibid., pp. 431–32.

Chapter Three

THE LIMITATIONS OF DENNETT'S ACCOUNT

In the final chapter of *CE* Dennett makes a clear statement of the task he has undertaken.

> I haven't replaced a metaphorical theory, the Cartesian Theater, with a nonmetaphorical ("literal, scientific") theory. All I have done, really, is to replace one family of metaphors and images with another, trading in the Theater, the Witness, the Central Meaner, the Figment, for Software, Virtual Machines, Multiple Drafts, a Pandemomium of Homunculi . . . metaphors are the tools of thought . . . it is important to equip yourself with the best set of tools available.[1]

Dennett makes an important point here, one that goes to the core of his project as a whole. What he is emphasizing is that metaphors are the "tools of thought." They are, for him, the means of accessing, negotiating, and interpreting the behavior of human animals in their social and physical world. His speculation prompts a critical question with regard to his own metaphors: Does his conception of human beings as narrative (and fictional) selves yield a more successful account of human behavior than other possible conceptions (for example, the conceptualization of them as Central Meaners, or as narrative, but nonfictional selves)? This chapter focuses on three core objections to Dennett's conceptualization of the narrative self: that it is unnecessarily narrow, and that it is epistemologically, and ontologically, fragile. I take each of these objections in turn.

THE LIMITS OF LANGUAGE

In his discussion of brain bifurcation, considered in chapter 2, Dennett's emphasis on narrative richness high-lights a significant weakness in his account. When he ignores data indicating that neural processes in the right hemisphere also causally contribute to a narrative account of the self, he places imaginative limits on the kind of narrative self it is possible to have. Significantly, the outcome of an operation that splits what may well be two sources of narrative selfhood has far more serious implications than the Dennettian account allows.

To put it briefly, language use enables humans to do all kinds of weird and wonderful things like imagining, anticipating, and evaluating; and also creating, communicating, and philosophizing. However, prioritizing linguistic ability in a hierarchy of features associated with selves has worrying consequences. First, it implies a judgment of inferiority toward those who cannot articulate for one reason or another.[2] Second, it has implications for all humans, articulate and nonarticulate, in that it implies a normative ranking of defining features of humanity where linguistic ability is at the top and abilities of an emotional, somatic, and spiritual kind are inevitably lower down. This puts an unnecessary and unwarranted limitation on the forms of expression and behavior that can count as uniquely important manifestations of humanity.

Happily, there are other contemporary theorists within the naturalist tradition who offer a more comprehensive account of the self than Dennett. I refer in particular to the work of Owen Flanagan and Antonio Damasio. First, both Flanagan and Damasio appeal to alternative accounts of consciousness to Dennett's as a basis for the expression of selfhood. Second, Flanagan extends the basis on which selves might be construed by arguing that the activities, practices, and projects of an individual's life might also support a sense of self.

In *Consciousness Reconsidered* and *Self Expressions*, Flanagan's model of the narrative self acknowledges that inarticulate emotional and spiritual features of human beings are also important aspects of human experience and should therefore be part of any adequate theory of the self. He tells the story of Jimmie, who, because he has Korsakoff's disease (the destruction of the mammiliary bodies in the brain from alcohol) has only a short-term memory.[3] Jimmie's experiences, according to Flanagan, do not connect in any meaningful way which might constitute a self, and he quotes Jimmie's psychologist Oliver Sacks, who describes

Jimmie's experiences as a kind of "Humean drivel."[4] However, Jimmie does seem to display a sense of self that is drawn from other sources—religion, art, music, and gardening:

> What sustained him [Jimmie] and his activity in these contexts was not so much a stream of his own bound by contentful memories but a stream of his own bound by affect, by mood, and by aesthetic, dramatic, and religious resonances.[5]

Flanagan claims "mood and affect, rather than memory, reconstitute Jimmie's stream, he feels alive, acts alive, and seems happy."[6] In this case, the streamlike quality of Jimmie's experience does not derive from an informational continuity based on memories, but an affective or emotional continuity.

In addition, Flanagan draws attention to other areas of human activity on which self-concepts can be based and thereby further underlines the thinness of the Dennettian account. In his objection to Charles Taylor's claim that an articulate self-comprehension and strong evaluation are necessary components of a rich and effective identity, Flanagan points out that Taylor's conception of personhood does not characterize many people.[7] This is because, for Flanagan, it posits linguistic competence as a condition of personhood and demands an evaluative capacity that is "heavily intellectualist."[8] He allows that while identity is "in large part linguistically created, sustained, and informed," not all self-interpretation needs verbalization.[9] In particular, Flanagan highlights the action-oriented mechanisms that can be sources of self-comprehension and motivation:

> But there is no incoherence whatsoever in thinking
> that identity and self-comprehension can accrue in
> environments that are relatively impoverished linguis-
> tically and by means of all manner of intrapersonal
> and extrapersonal feedback mechanisms: by way of
> feelings of coordination, integration, and integrity, of
> fit with the social world mediated by the body lan-
> guage of others, and so on. Such self-comprehension
> might involve an evolving sense of who one is, of what
> is important to oneself, and of how one wants to live
> one's life.[10]

The advantage he sees with the narrative metaphor is
that it construes the self as the location of what "one perceives as most important, what one cares most about."[11]
This need not be revealed by first-person articulation but
by "the cares, concerns, and projects as revealed in how
the person lives."[12] This kind of identity is established
through a strong identification with "something or
someone—baseball, sophistication, concern for the fate
of grass or one's teammates."[13] Where Taylor's formulation focuses on reflection and evaluation, Flanagan's formulation focuses on "the strength of one's identification—to absorption in some end or ends, whatever that
end or those ends might be."[14] With Jimmie for instance,
it is the garden or religious practice.

What Flanagan appeals to as a basis for the self is a
stream of consciousness that is very different from the
kind of consciousness that Dennett imagines as a virtual

machine—his MDM. The latter account of consciousness emphasizes its discontinuity, impersonal nature, and
reportability (in multiple drafts). As such, the MDM can
only support and explain a particular account of the self
as a narrative fiction. The point is that when Flanagan
describes a certain kind of human behavior and explains
it by postulating a particular kind of continuity of consciousness, he is providing evidence that the notion of
consciousness is not as easily captured, articulated, and
explained as Dennett might lead one to believe. Flanagan
distinguishes between two kinds of self-consciousness,
or two kinds of selves that are generated by our stream-
like experiences: the indexical "I" and the narrative self.
Short-term memory is ground for the "bare, pathetic, thin
subject" of the self-referential "I."[15] This is self-conscious
experience in the sense that "there is something it is like
for the subject to have that experience . . . that it happens
to her, occurs in her stream."[16] Long-term memory offers
a personal identity in the "rich thick sense of knowing
who one is and where one is coming from."[17] This is a
higher-order model of the self that Flanagan calls a Self-
Represented Identity (SRI). What accounts for a person's
sense of privacy and individuality for Flanagan is the fact
that they are constituted by a unique stream of experience. What counts at any one time as "me" is the result of
the coming together of those events in my stream that I
most care about. Flanagan identifies forward planning,
goal setting, and fighting for ends as functions of consciousness and concludes that: "The senses of identity,
direction, agency, and a life plan are all grounded in the
memorable connections of the stream."[18]

Even if one accepts the MDM as a good empirical explanation of some kinds of conscious behavior, it does not exhaust all of what is meant by the term. Kathleen Wilkes, for example, who agrees with Dennett that consciousness does not pick out a natural kind or thing, nevertheless claims that there are several categories into which the notion of consciousness can be divided. Like Dennett, she claims "there is no 'thing' which is consciousness—no unitary or special capacity or state of mind."[19]

> Put another way, "consciousness" does not pick out a natural kind, does not refer to the sort of thing that has a "nature" appropriate for scientific study, or which can constitute a "joint" into which nature is to be carved by the sciences. (Nor do "carpet" or "calendar," and for precisely analogous reasons.) So there may be no helpful or substantial generalizations about human consciousness wherewith to aid our study of the person via the study of *homo sapiens*.[20]

She offers a fine grained analysis of consciousness as an adjective that can be ascribed to a "heterogeneous bunch of things" of which Wilkes claims there are several distinguishable kinds.[21] In sum, if consciousness is not a *thing,* then consciousness is not a *single thing*, and the MDM is one of a number of possible models of consciousness. Incidentally, I do not think that this is inconsistent with Dennett's overall position because he himself offers alternatives to the MDM, but it does challenge the emphasis he places on *one* kind of consciousness as a basis for self-concepts.

However, problems with the Dennettian account of the narrative self cannot be completely addressed by describing the phenomenon of consciousness more comprehensively. This is because consciousness, however it is described, makes only a partial contribution to the explanation of self-concepts. If, *like* Dennett, one accepts that neuroscientific research can contribute to explanations of why humans evolve into the kind of selves they do, and if, *unlike* Dennett, one does not exclude any data on the basis of any a priori decisions made about what should and should not matter in regard to the self, then one should pay close attention to all of the research that is emerging and not just specific kinds of consciousness research.

There is a growing body of opinion which challenges the assumption that the neural processes most relevant to the construction of the self are those associated with the left hemisphere of the brain.[22] Antonio Damasio, a leading neuroscientist, has claimed that while language largely depends on left hemisphere structures, the right hemisphere has a preferential involvement in processing emotion and representations of body states. Damasio distinguishes between the non-verbal "core self" and the verbal "autobiographical self" in order to underline his view that we are selves whether or not we have language.[23] His account of the narrative self is more inclusive than Dennett's because it allows for the idea of a non-verbal story teller. His idea is that even before we have language, our brains are already drawing maps of a kind, which register what is happening to us, around us and in us.

Wordless storytelling is natural. . . . Telling stories, in the sense of registering what happens in the form of brain maps, is probably a brain obsession and probably begins relatively early both in terms of evolution and in terms of the complexity of the neural structures required to create narratives. Telling stories precedes language, since it is, in fact, a condition for language, and it is based not just in the cerebral cortex but elsewhere in the brain and in the right hemisphere as well as the left.[24]

Damiso attempts a fine-grained analysis of emotions and distinguishes between three kinds: (1) innate or primary emotions such as fear or anger which are hardwired as responses to certain stimuli in the environment or in bodies such as reptilian types of movements or growling sounds; (2) adult or secondary emotions such as euphoria and ecstasy, melancholy and wistfulness, panic and shyness which occur once humans begin forming evaluative connections between different kinds of objects and situations and the engagement of primary emotions; and (3) background feelings which Damasio calls "the feeling of life itself, the sense of being."[25] It is the latter that Damasio associates with the human sense of self:

In all probability it is these feelings, rather than emotional ones, that we experience most frequently in a lifetime. We are only subtly aware of a background feeling, but aware enough to be able to report instantly on its quality. A background feeling is not what we feel when we jump out of our skin for sheer joy, or when we are despondent over lost love; both of these actions correspond to emotional body states. A background feeling corresponds instead to the body state prevailing *between* emotions. . . . The background feeling is our image of the body landscape when it is not shaken by emotion. . . . I submit that without them the very core of your representation of self would be broken.[26]

These background feelings generate a sense of continuity and unity not derived from conscious memory or verbal reports of past doings or future plans. Rather, it is located in the largely inarticulate right hemisphere. It is the right hemisphere that maps the general body structure through proprioception (sense of our muscles and joints) and interoception (sense of our viscera). These constitute an image of what one's body tends to be like generally, rather than what it is like right now.

Unlike our environment, whose constitution does change, and unlike the images we construct relative to that environment, which are fragmentary and conditioned by external circumstance, background feeling is mostly about body states. Our individual identity is anchored on this island of illusory living sameness against which we can be aware of myriad other things that manifestly change around the organism.[27]

When things go wrong with the right hemisphere, things can go terribly wrong for the individual. One example is the condition of anosognosia which can accompany certain patterns of brain damage to the right hemisphere that cause paralysis on the left side.[28] The problem for

anosognosiacs—those who deny that they have an illness or disease—according to Damasio, is that they
cannot avail of information about their current body
image and so cannot update their representation of their
bodies.[29] They fail to recognize that the reality of their
body landscape has changed. The conditions usually
associated with personal identity are in place: they
remember who they are, where they live and worked,
who their friends are. And yet, none of this information
impacts on their perception of themselves. They are
unaware that they are, for example, paralyzed; they are
uninterested in the consequences, unconcerned about
the future, and emotionally flat. Without constant
updating, they are caught in the past.

While Damasio, like Dennett, posits the brain as a survival tool to which culture has added further strategies,
he is unlike Dennett in his evaluation of the relationship
between verbalization and selfhood. While Damasio
allows that the ability to verbalize might be included as
an important feature of the self, he does not consider that
it is a necessary condition of there being a self. For him,
"we are, and then we think, and we think only inasmuch
as we are."[30] Importantly, for Damasio, emotional states,
modified by life's experience, act as what he calls
"somatic markers" to inhibit certain clusters of thoughts
and maintain others in attention.[31] This is his account of
why the task of reasoning ends when it ends. He cites the
findings of research involving patients whose frontal cortical regions were impaired, thereby disrupting the
neural pathways connecting emotional and decision
making processes. These patients are rational decision

makers extraordinaire (akin to the ideal thinkers of philosophy), but they do not have normal emotional responses and are unable to live safely and successfully in the real world.[32] These rationalizers need what Jimmie, as portrayed by Flanagan, has—emotional response and continuity—and have in abundance what Jimmie lacks: reasoning and memory.

EPISTEMOLOGICAL FRAGILITY

Dennett underlines the epistemological fragility of his narrative theory of the self by acknowledging that there are difficulties adjudicating between true and false narrative selves at any one time and determining the conditions of their identity over time. He argues that all "normal" selves are milder forms of pathological cases; we are all "inveterate and inventive autobiographical novelists [we are] confabulators, telling and retelling ourselves the story of our own lives, with scant attention to the question of truth."[33] He concludes from this that the only status and stability the narrative self can maintain is derived from the beliefs that constitute it, without which the self lapses for a period of time or for good:

> [S]elves are not independently existing soul-pearls, but artifacts, subject to sudden shifts in status. The only "momentum" that accrues to the trajectory of a self, or a club, is the stability imparted to it by the web of beliefs that constitute it, and when those beliefs lapse, it lapses, either permanently or temporarily. [34]

On one occasion in *CE*, Dennett likens his account of the narrative self to a Derridean deconstructionist account of the self. He quotes a passage from a novel that he has read to illustrate the deconstructionist view, which posits the self as "only a subject position in an infinite web of discourses—the discourses of power, sex, family, science, religion, poetry, etc."[35] However well or ill Dennett understands the deconstructionist project, he likens his own thesis to it with the intention of highlighting the deconstruction of the substantial notion of the self that his own theory is intended to achieve.

One implication of construing the self in this way is the difficulty of determining how it persists in time; there seems to be no evident means of determining whether the fictional self at time T2 is the same self at time T1. Indeed, Dennett might respond to such a difficulty by claiming that there are no sure ways of individuating fictions, nor need there be. In sum, one's autobiography may or may not be truthful to the historical events that occurred in one's lifetime, which means that there is no way of determining whether, from a first-person point of view, you are the same person as the kindergarten adventurer of your memory:

> [W]e saw that while consciousness appears to be continuous, in fact it is gappy. A self could be just as gappy, lapsing into nothingness as easily as a candle flame is snuffed, only to be rekindled at some later time, under more auspicious circumstances. Are you the very person whose kindergarten adventures you sketchily recall (sometimes vividly, sometimes dimly)? Are the adventures of that child, whose trajectory

through space and time has apparently been continuous with the trajectory of your body, your very own adventures?[36]

Even so, I think that Dennett has some room to maneuver here. His and Humphrey's discussion on people with multiple personalities, for example, places a particular stress on the role of others in the constitution of the self:[37]

In very much a parallel way, [to the way in which the media moulds Presidential candidates] we suggest, a human being first creates—unconsciously—one or more ideal fictive-selves and then elects the best supported of these into office as her Head of Mind. A significant difference in the human case, however, is that there is likely to be considerably more *outside influence*. Parents, friends, and even enemies may all contribute to the image of "what it means to be me," as well as—and maybe over and above—the internal news media.[38]

Not only do others contribute to how an individual sees themselves; they also give weight to the credibility of any autobiographical account. It is clear from the criterion determining the status of cases of multiple personality, laid down by Humphrey and Dennett, that for any given personality to be considered a "fully fledged" self, others with whom she interacts would have to be convinced by her rhetoric about herself.[39] If applied to conflicting accounts of the self in general, this criterion affords Dennett a means of deciding among them, because it suggests that any given personal account of the self can be tested against the accounts of others. The question remains what such a test would involve, but here are some suggestions.

First, such a test could involve measuring any personal biographical account against the historically recorded events of that person's life. While Dennett raises doubts about the kind of certainty one can have regarding one's childhood adventures, he explicitly rejects a claim that he attributes to Derrida—that there is nothing outside of the text—on the grounds that there are bookcases, buildings, bodies, and bacteria.[40] And he further adds that there are "facts of the matter" such as whether or not historical events actually took place:

> There *is* a fact of the matter about whether Oswald and Ruby were in cahoots, even if it forever eludes investigation. It is not *just* a matter of which story plays well to which audiences, and I would say the same about all such quarries of empirical investigation.[41]

Second, such a test could include the idea that any given account of the self must be consistent with the general behavior of the individual involved. For example, I might reject as false the claim by a reader of this text that he is a high-wire acrobat on the grounds that such an activity does not cohere (easily) with his current philosophizing activity. Such an epistemic standard is in keeping with Dennett's naturalist commitments generally. On this reading, the concept of the self as a center of narrative gravity is best understood as a model of the self, made grave, if you like, by standards of intersubjective acceptability such as the constraints of historical documentation and consistency. Such a self is fictional in the sense that it does not directly refer to a set of underlying features, but it is not wholly arbitrary because it is constrained by such things as the testimony of others, historical documents, and the degree to which it helps to explain the behavior of the individual concerned and predict what she will do.

A further constraint could appeal to the more realist tendencies of the HM, namely, the second feature of the HM that tests first-person reports or narratives against available objectively discovered data. This would involve testing personal narratives against what was actually happening from a neurophysiological point of view to the organism in question. This constraint would, of course, draw Dennett further away from his initial commitment to mild realism and closer to a more eliminative materialist position regarding psychological categories. However, if Dennett is to address the epistemological frailty of his account of the narrative self while remaining within the parameters of a scientific world-view, then this is one move he could reluctantly make.

ONTOLOGICAL FRAGILITY

Dennett's account of the fictional self rests primarily on his initial unraveling of the concept of consciousness. As outlined in chapter 1, he rejects the Cartesian conclusion that because conscious experience involves a point of view, such a point of view must presuppose an observer or self with a determinate identity and defining features such as unity and continuity. So far, so good. The attempt to refigure consciousness and unravel the implications of such a refiguration for the status of the self is a move that a number of philosophers have made. However, Dennett's alternative to the idea of consciousness as "Cartesian Theater" and the self as real is to construe conscious and unconscious brain processes as a Multiple Draft "virtual machine" and the self as a fiction.[42] Dennett disposes of one objectivist view of consciousness—as a unity—only to replace it with a second objectivist view of consciousness—as fragmented. What is common to both is an emphasis on the objectivist view.

Dennett's privileging of objectivist scientific methodologies in the HM means that the world he is interested in is a world that is ultimately populated by scientifically determinable and measurable entities (such as atoms or brains), abstractions (such as gravity and triangles), or actions (such as combustion or neurotransmitters firing). When Dennett runs out of scientific entities, he opts for the third person stance: intentional, physical, and design. On this view, the self is real only insofar as it contributes to scientifically relevant modes of explanation. Thus, Dennett is lead to reject the Cartesian idea that the self is real and adopt the idea of a fictional and impoverished self that is real only insofar as it is useful (in other words, that its deployment contributes to the successful prediction of human behavior). The claim that the concept of the self is useful (and therefore real) because of its predictive power seems profoundly counter-intuitive and supports our usual sense of being a self only at the cost of greatly reducing its intelligibility. Granted that the scientific view of explanatory success is that any given explanation should have predictive power, the question arises in relation to our sense of self as to whether or not such a model of explanation is sufficiently comprehensive. After all, when we think of one another as selves, is it for the purpose, simply of predicting behavior as economists or advertisers might? Think of the complex nature and texture of human life—our relationships with loved ones, our responsibilities, regrets, successes, dreams and promises. The scientific explanation of selfhood, as construed by Dennett, drastically reduces the contribution it can make to rendering all of this intelligible.

In effect, Dennett's concept of the narrative self could be described as ontologically fragile. What I mean by this is that, first, the Dennettian self is not real in the way that scientifically defined objects are real. Second, whatever status it does have derives from its role in intentional or design accounts of human behavior, and this radically reduces its capacity to render the breadth and depth of human experience and behavior intelligible.

NATURALISM AND PHENOMENOLOGY

In sum, Dennett's strategy in relation to the self involves the adoption of the HM and the subsequent rejection of the Cartesian account of consciousness. The question that arises here is: how useful is such a strategy as a means of understanding what it is the concept of self tries to capture? Given that Dennett directly compares the bracketing of the HM with the bracketing of Husserl's *epoché*, it is worthwhile taking a brief look at what Husserl is trying to do. The latter, like Dennett, eschews Cartesianism but, unlike Dennett, does not embrace a naturalist view of the world. Husserl's account of consciousness in the first two *Cartesian Meditations* holds on to Descartes' idea that we cannot have certain knowledge of the external world but rejects the Cartesian skeptical conclusion that it must follow from this that all our conceptions of the world ought to be placed in doubt.[43] Husserl rejects what I call the *realist thesis* adopted by Descartes as a response to the skepticism that he thought must inevitably follow his account of subjectivity. The following is a crude summary of the realist thesis:

1. there is a distinction between the subject of perception and the world that he perceives;
2. the philosopher's task is to, somehow, forge links between what appears to the subject of experience and what supposedly lies behind these appearances in order to assess how and under what conditions subjective perceptions and judgments about the world are true of the world;[44]
3. The task might be achieved by postulating relations of resemblance and causality between the subject and the world—the subject is posited as having mental pictures resembling objects in the world that cause them.

Husserl rejects the realist thesis; in particular, he rejects the idea that there is a mind-independent world of objects that must somehow be accessed through the correct application of human consciousness. Calling it a "naïve objectivism," he argues instead that, on his account of consciousness, there are no private experiences on the one hand, and publicly accessible objects on the other.[45] He understands consciousness as intentional; it is not consciousness of a representation of something (as Descartes would have it), it is consciousness *of* or *about* the thing itself. He shifts emphasis from the Cartesian idea of the conscious subject on the inside and the world on the outside to the idea of consciousness as a relation with the world, as a mode through which the world opens up to certain kinds of beings.[46] On his account, judgments based on common sense or scientific and philosophical frameworks about the mind-independent existence of objects have to be suspended or bracketed. Instead, the phenomenologist's task involves a full description of what is presented to conscious experience in everyday life. For example, in a phenomenological analysis of the operation of consciousness of a tree, what gets prioritized is the experience of seeing (or touching, or climbing) a tree, not the puzzle of linking consciousness on the one side with a tree on the other, nor the puzzle of establishing whether the tree "really" exists or not. Significantly, the activity of consciousness is understood as being oriented toward the world in multiple ways—conscious human beings perceive, but they also imagine, feel, will, believe, fear, resist, desire, and value.

Dennett's particular brand of naturalism expressed in the HM, however, ignores the implications that phenomenology has for the privileged status of the scientific world view and conflates the phenomenological account of intentional conscious experience with a psychological account of experience. First, while Dennett accepts the advantages of the *epoché* in so far as it is intended to avoid the distortion and distraction of ontological assumptions; he and Husserl have very different views of the role that science ultimately plays in our understanding of the world. For Husserl, one consequence of the intentional nature of consciousness is that it undermines Cartesian-inspired scientific discourses that privilege third-person accounts of the world over phenomenological description and deem the objects determined by the methods and standards of science as the only real objects. The argument is well made by the phenomenologist Maurice Merleau-Ponty who argues that scientific explanation is parasitic on phenomenological description and that the latter should be prioritized over the former:

> The whole universe of science is built upon the world as directly experienced, and if we want to subject science itself to rigorous scrutiny and arrive at a precise assessment of its meaning and scope, we must begin by re-awakening the basic experience of the world of which science is the second-order expression. . . . Scientific points of view, according to which my existence is a moment of the world's, are always both naïve and at the same time dishonest, because they take for granted, without explicitly mentioning it, the other point of view, namely that of consciousness,

through which from the outset a world forms itself
around me and begins to exist for me.[47]

For Husserl and Merleau-Ponty, phenomenological
description of the world is the foundation on which any
theory of the world, including scientific theory, must be
founded; but for Dennett, the world as revealed by science is privileged. Even though he, like Husserl, seems, at
least initially, to eschew scientific realism, he nevertheless privileges scientific methodology when he adopts
the objectivist stance of the HM.

If the phenomenological step back is justified, the
question that arises is as follows: What are the grounds
for Dennett's privileging of the objectivist stance as a
mode of accessing the world? According to one of Dennett's critics, David Thompson, there are no grounds: that
Dennett simply refuses to apply the *epoché* to the scientific world view and thus leaves it without warrant or
foundation.[48]

> Dennett frequently writes as if scientists had a god's-
> eye view of the world, as if they could know things-in-
> themselves, things as they are in absolute independ-
> ence from the meanings that human knowers set up.
> But his pandemonic account of the production of
> speech (or writing), for example, must apply to scien-
> tific discourse as it does to any other discourse. . . .
> Husserl applies the *epoché* to all experience, including
> scientific experience. Insofar as *Consciousness
> Explained* neglects to make the equivalent move, it
> leaves science as a kind of skyhook without founda-
> tion, to invert a metaphor.[49]

Thompson further claims that *Consciousness Explained* studies consciousness for its own sake while taking science for granted," while "Husserl investigates consciousness in order to establish a sold foundation for science."[50] However, Dennett's response to any worry concerning his privileging of science is to claim that whatever scientific assumptions he takes for granted are "innocent."[51] By this he means to indicate that given his primary aim to develop a theory of consciousness, his scientific assumptions are warranted if they neither "blind [him] to important truths" nor require radical revision once he has achieved his goal.[52] He distinguishes his approach from Husserl's with the claim that he is not convinced that the phenomenological method is equally "innocent" because he argues that it might inflate and distort the phenomena of consciousness.[53]

The question that arises then is which of the two viewpoints, phenomenological or scientific, is the more innocent? I would argue in favor of the former. This is because when Dennett treats first-person conscious experience solely as psychological experience and distinguishes between lies and truth, clarity and confusion, by appealing to scientifically determined criteria, he is putting theory before description. This is because the identification and correction of errors of perception is not what is at stake in the phenomenological emphasis on conscious experience. The subject of conscious experience is not, for Husserl, simply a psychological entity who may be confused about the way the world is. Instead, he posits the subject of consciousness as a Transcendental Ego, not a thinking *thing*. For Husserl, anticipating Dennett, once

Descartes arrived at "I exist," he made the fateful error of substantiating the *cogito*: "Descartes introduced the apparently insignificant but actually fateful change whereby the ego becomes a substantia *cogitans*, a separate human "*mens sive animus*" [mind or soul]."[54] Husserl argues that the subject of perception cannot itself be part of the world of perception. Instead, the subject is cast as the Transcendental Ego: an entity which must be presupposed as a condition for any perception of the world to be possible and for any claims about its existence to be intelligible.[55] As a necessary condition of meaning, the Ego is distinguished from the subject considered as a member of a natural species and the subject considered as a psychological entity: "This Ego, with his Ego-life, who necessarily remains for me, by virtue of such *epoché,* is not a piece of the world; and if he says, "I exist, *ego cogito,*" that no longer signifies, "I, this man, exists" . . . Nor am I the separately considered psyche itself."[56] So, for Husserl, the Ego is not a psychological entity whose subjective experience and observations about the world may be unreliable and in need of correction by objective methods. Instead, the Ego is a fundamental feature of human life and plays a more foundational role in the relationship between human beings and the world than either Descartes or Dennett envisage. The distance between a phenomenological account of consciousness and a psychological one is made even more clear in the later Husserl, in particular in *The Crisis of European Sciences and Transcendental Phenomenology,* where his idea of the Ego as a pure consciousness is reconceived as a historically embedded and embodied consciousness. [57]

Concerns about the precise status of and warrant for the Transcendental Ego have occupied any number of Husserlian scholars and critics since it was first mooted by Husserl.[58] However, I will not pursue these concerns here because my interest lies solely in the implications that Husserl's work has for Dennett's position. In short, if we accept Husserl's account of consciousness and the *epoché* as a metaphysical rather than a psychological thesis, then no particular discourse about the way the world is can be automatically privileged, because no discourse cuts the world up at its joints. Dennett will have to provide warrant for his naturalist stance.

What is at stake in this debate about the privileging, or otherwise, of the phenomenological stance over the objectivist stance is the implication that such privileging has for understanding the concept of self and whatever we think it refers or captures. For example, given Dennett's privileging of scientific explanations of human life, he posits a particular account of the self as a fictional narrative. Alternatively, Husserl's phenomenological step back leaves the way open for any number of discourses (such as psychology, literature, philosophy, history, and anthropology, as well as the biological and neurosciences) to contribute to conceptualizations of selfhood. It is this approach, adopted by Paul Ricoeur and discussed in the following chapters, that enables the latter to develop a very different account of the self as narrative.

I have indicated that there are limitations to Dennett's account of the self: its reliance on linguistic capacities and its epistemological, and ontological, fragility. The fact that Dennett's application of the HM to the problem of the self has not produced an adequate theory of the self challenges other naturalist philosophers to do better. Indeed, there are other naturalist philosophers such as Flanagan and Damasio who, like Dennett, want to disavow Cartesianism while retaining the language of the self, but who, unlike Dennett, relate concepts of the self to alternative models of consciousness and a larger range of human activities. In addition, I have suggested ways in which the epistemological fragility of the Dennettian account of the narrative self can be ameliorated. Even so, the inadequacies of the Dennettian model also suggest that philosophers who appeal to the natural sciences are looking in the wrong direction for descriptive categories, epistemological standards, and theoretical frameworks that can do justice to the very complex notion of the self. This is because Dennett's commitment to the objectivist stance of naturalism forces him to explain the phenomenon of "consciousness" and experiences of subjectivity in terms of an objectivist perspective. While the latter leads him to disavow the Cartesian idea that the self is real, it also encourages him to espouse the idea of a fictional and impoverished self that fails all the intuitive criteria of selfhood. In addition, because Dennett measures success in terms of the achievement of scientific objectives, the explanatory usefulness of even theoretical fictions, such as the narrative self, is measured solely on their predictive power. Dennett's commitment to naturalist methodologies and standards seems inevitably to lead to an account of a very fragile self with a drastically reduced role in making human life intelligible.

Prompted by this unsatisfactory outcome, the fol-

lowing chapters will engage with Paul Ricoeur's phenomenological-hermeneutic perspective to provide an
alternative to naturalist inspired accounts of the self. In
the course of my exploration, I pay attention to some of
the problems that have been identified with Dennett's
account. In particular, I will decide whether or not
Ricoeur's alternative approach adequately addresses
worries that conceiving the self narratively exaggerates
the relationship between selfhood and linguistic ability
and entails a notion of selfhood that is epistemologically
and ontologically suspect.

NOTES TO CHAPTER 3

1. Dennett, *CE*, p. 455.

2. There has been debate on the countability of Dennett's mind(s) and the moral implications of his claim. See, for
example, Roland Puccetti's target article, "Dennett on the Split-
Brain," *Psycoloquy* 4, no. 52 (1993), http://psycprints.ecs.soton
.ac.uk/archive/00000377/ (accessed August 14, 2006) and Puccetti's reply to critics in "Narrative Richness as a Necessary
Condition for the Self," *Psycoloquy* 5, no. 18 (1994), http://psy-
cprints.ecs.soton.ac.uk/archive/00000377/ (accessed August
14, 2006). See also Valerie Gray Hardcastle, "A New Agenda for
Studying Consciousness, Commentary on Puccetti on Split-
Brain," *Psycoloquy* 4, no. 57 (1993), http://psycprints.ecs.soton
.ac.uk/archive/00000351/ (accessed August 14, 2006).

3. Owen Flanagan, *Consciousness Reconsidered* (Cambridge, MA: MIT Press, 1994) and *Self Expressions* (Oxford:
Oxford University Press, 1996).

4. Flanagan, *Consciousness Reconsidered*, p. 168.

5. Ibid.

6. Ibid.

7. Charles Taylor, *Sources of the Self: The Making of Modern Identity* (Cambridge, MA: Harvard University Press, 1989) and "What is Human Agency?" in *The Self: Psychological and Philosophical Issues*, ed. T. Mischel (Oxford: Basil Blackwell, 1977).

8. Flanagan, *Self Expressions*, p. 157.

9. Ibid., p. 155.

10. Ibid., p. 156.

11. Ibid., p. 158.

12. Ibid.

13. Ibid., pp. 158–59.

14. Ibid., p. 159.

15. Flanagan, *Consciousness Reconsidered*, p. 155.

16. Ibid., p. 194.

17. Ibid., p. 144.

18. Ibid., pp. 166–7.

19. Kathleen Wilkes, *Real People* (Oxford: Clarendon Press, 1994), p. 193.

20. Ibid.

21. Ibid., p. 168.

22. The Russian psychologist Alexander Romanovich Luria is associated with the development of neuropsychology, which attempts to map the complex relations between neural states and mental states. Luria emphasizes the importance for psychology of qualitative research, or the recounting of the stories and biographies of patients as distinct from the impersonal approach of neurological science. His book, *Higher Cortical Functions in Man,* trans. Basil Haigh (New York: Basic Books, 1980), explores the functions of the left hemisphere of the brain and identifies the behavioral changes that follow on various lesions occurring in the

left hemisphere. Most studies since Luria have focused on the functions of the left hemisphere.

In an attempt to redress the balance, Oliver Sacks (whose patient, Jimmie, was the subject of the earlier discussion with regard to Owen Flanagan) in *The Man Who Mistook His Wife For a Hat* (London: Duckworth, 1985), focuses on the effects that follow lesions to the right hemisphere. Following Luria, Sacks claims that first-person reports of personal experiences and the patient's own biography make an important contribution to the understanding of what is involved or required in the construction of personal identity. Sacks suggests that the peculiar nature of right-hemisphere syndromes might be addressed by a new sort of neurology which would explore the physical foundations of selfhood.

23. Antonio R. Damasio, *The Feeling of What Happens* (London: Vintage, 2000), pp. 174–233.

24. Ibid., pp. 188–89.

25. Antonio R. Damasio, *Descartes' Error* (London: Macmillan/ Papermac, 1996), p. 150.

26. Ibid., p. 151.

27. Ibid., p. 155.

28. This region in the right hemisphere cortical area of the brain is known as the somatosensory system and, according to Damasio, it generates the "most comprehensive and integrated map of the current body state available to the brain" (Ibid., p. 66).

29. The term *anosognosia* comes from the Greek *nosos*, meaning "disease," and *gnosis*, meaning "knowledge" and denotes the inability to acknowledge disease in oneself (ibid., p. 62).

30. Ibid., p. 248.

31. Ibid., p. 173.

32. Ibid., pp. 173–201.

33. Dennett, "Why everyone is a novelist," p. 1028

34. Dennett, *CE*, p. 423.

35. Ibid., pp. 410–11. In *CE* Dennett does not indicate that he has actually read the original texts of any deconstructionist philosophers. He introduces this view of Derrida's position as it is expressed by a character in David Lodge's novel *Nice Work* (London: Secker and Warberg, 1988). However, elsewhere, though still not indicating that he has actually read any of the deconstructionists, he is far more scathing of their work: "[F]or pomposity, deliberate obscurity, and just plain silliness, I know of nothing to compare with the deconstructionists" ("Dennett and Carr Further Explained: an Exchange," Emory Cognition Project Report, no. 28 [Department of Psychology, Emory University, April 1994], p. 2. Also titled "Tiptoeing past the Covered Wagons," http://cogprints .org/278/00/tiptoe.htm [accessed August 14, 2006]). For similar declarations, see also Dennett, "Postmodernism and Truth," paper delivered at World Congress of Philosophy, August 13, 1998, http://www.butterfliesandwheels.com/articleprint.php?num=13 (accessed August 14, 2006).

36. Dennett, *CE*, p. 423.

37. See chapter 2 of this book, "Puzzle cases."

38. Humphrey and Dennett, "Speaking for Our Selves," p. 41.

39. Incidentally, this intersubjective dimension of the narrative self draws Dennett's account closer to the phenomenological account of Paul Ricoeur, which I discuss in chapter 4.

40. Dennett, *CE*, p. 411. Note that Dennett is deliberately playful in his treatment of the position he attributes to Jacques Derrida. It is likely, in my view, that Dennett has never paid any serious attention to the actual Derridean position on the subject. If he had, he would know that Derrida's position with regard to the subject is neither as naïve nor as simple as he presents it. However, that is another debate into which I cannot enter here.

41. Daniel Dennett, "Back from the Drawing Board," p. 234.

42. Dennett, *CE*, p. 455.

43. Edmund Husserl, *Cartesian Meditations*, trans. Dorion Cairns (The Hague: Martinus Nijhoff, 1960).

44. The phenomenologist and realist deployments of the term "phenomenon" should not be confused. For the former, a phenomenal object is an object of experience; for example, it is a table, chair, or kiss as it is perceived, touched, or resisted by an experiencer. For the latter, a phenomenon is the appearance of some feature of underlying reality; for example, a table, understood as phenomenon, is an appearance that represents or misrepresents some genuine feature of the world.

45. Edmund Husserl, *Cartesian Meditations*, p. 4.

46. Ricoeur, whose philosophical position is explored later in this book, has the following to say about intentionality:

The great advance of phenomenology was to reject the containing/contained relationship that made the psyche a place. . . . Intentionality introduces the notion of transcendent purpose. . . . I am outside myself when I see, which is to say that seeing consists in being confronted by something that is not myself, and therefore participating in an external world. I would say therefore that consciousness is not a closed place, about which I might wonder how something enters it from outside, because it is, now and always, outside of itself (Paul Ricoeur, *The Just*, trans. David Pellauer [Chicago: University of Chicago Press, 2000], pp. 119–120).

47. Maurice Merleau-Ponty, *Phenomenology of Perception*, trans. Colin Smith (London: Routledge and Kegan Paul, 1981), pp. viii–ix.

48. As far as I know, this criticism was first made by Carr in 1998 (David Carr, "Phenomenology and Fiction in Dennett," *International Journal of Philosophical Studies* 6, no. 3, (1998): 338.

49. David L. Thompson, "Phenomenology and Heterophenomenology: Husserl and Dennett on Reality and Science," in *Dennett's Philosophy, A Comprehensive Assessment*, ed. Don Ross, Andrew Brook, David Thompson (Cambridge, MA: MIT Press, 2000), p. 209.

50. Ibid., p. 202.

51. Daniel Dennett, "With a Little Help From My Friends," p. 362.

52. Ibid.

53. Ibid., pp. 362–63.

54. Husserl, *Cartesian Meditations*, p. 24.

55. Ibid.

56. Ibid., p. 25.

57. See Edmund Husserl, *The Crisis of European Sciences and Transcendental Phenomenology*, trans. David Carr (Evanston: Northwestern University Press, 1970), sec. 15, where he explores the way in which the *epoché* itself is historically constituted; and ibid., sec. 43, where he connects consciousness more intimately with the world of experience or "life-world" (*Lebenswelt*).

58. See also *Husserl: Expositions and Appraisals*.

Chapter Four

CONFRONTING NATURALISM

In *Oneself as Another* (*OA*), the concluding section of *Time and Narrative* vol. 3 (*TN3*), and his more recent essays, the French philosopher, Paul Ricoeur, lays out his account of the self.[1] What he and Dennett have in common is that they both conceive of the self in narrative terms. However, what pivotally distinguishes their approaches to the problem of the self is that, as already discussed, Dennett is a naturalist who privileges the language and standards of scientific explanation, while Ricoeur is a phenomenologist who privileges the language of lived experience and the standards of hermeneutic interpretation. This difference leads them to view the relationship of the narrative self to truth and knowledge according to radically different criteria.

Briefly, Ricoeur argues that any account of our sense of self involves a detour through available cultural and historical discourses. Moreover, it is constrained by certain basic conditions of human existence: reflexivity, corporeality, intentionality, temporality, and intersubjec-

tivity.[2] Following on this, he rejects the Cartesian notion
of the self as a thing-like unity (call it the *real self*) and,
instead, views the self as a unity of action (call it the
capable self).[3] Ricoeur's thesis is that his account of the
capable self as a culturally mediated unity of action best
reflects the basic conditions of human existence. He
argues that its unity and continuity can be determined in
a number of ways. In particular, for my purposes, he
unravels the way it is narratively identified.[4] I engage
with Ricoeur's account of the capable self and its narrative identity in the following chapters, but first, I will discuss his theoretical starting point: the graft between phenomenology and hermeneutics.

PHENOMENOLOGY AND HERMENEUTICS

Writing in 1995, Ricoeur describes his philosophical task
with regard to the self as a "grafting" of hermeneutics onto
phenomenology.[5] Unlike Dennett, whose relationship
with phenomenology, as indicated in the last chapter, is
confused and half-hearted, Ricoeur takes the phenomenological step back seriously. Before I engage with Ricoeur's
treatment of the Husserlian enterprise, however, there is
one objection to Husserl's position that I will briefly summarize because it explains why Ricoeur, along with
others, was keen on grafting phenomenology with
hermeneutics. One objection that can be leveled at phenomenology that is associated with Ludwig Wittgenstein,

and analytic philosophy generally, is that the phenomenological privileging of direct experience overlooks the
importance of language as the basis on which experience
is made meaningful. For many analytic philosophers, especially Wittgenstein in the *Tractatus*, linguistic structures
map directly onto the real world, and it follows from this
that it is the analysis of language, not direct experience,
which is deemed by him to be the proper task of philosophy.[6] Granted the privileging of language on this view,
the standards of excellence against which conflicting theories about the world are evaluated include logical techniques, clarity of concepts, rigor, and precision.

However, an alternative approach, which attempts to
ease the tension between language on the one hand and
experience on the other, is that of hermeneutic philosophy: the theory and practice of interpretation. The
term "hermeneutic" has its roots in the Greek verb
hermeneuein, meaning "to interpret," and the noun
hermeneia, meaning "interpretation."[7] It was addressed
as a subject by a number of ancient writers, including
Plato, Plutarch, Euripides, Lucretius, and, in particular,
Aristotle in *De Interpretatione*.[8] The hermeneutic tradition in its modern form has its roots in the 17th-century
need for rules governing the proper exegesis of Biblical
texts. This need arose because of the absence of a cen-
tralized authority within the Protestant Church to guar-
antee the "correct" meanings of scripture. It first
appeared as a book title in 1654: *Hermeutica Sacra Sive
Methodus Exponendarum Sacrarum Litterarum*, by J.
C. Dannhauer.[9] In the 19th century, the hermeneutic
approach was applied to elicit or recover the hidden

meanings of obscure or symbolic nonbiblical texts. Later, however, hermeneutics was given an extended and more philosophically interesting role as a critical methodology for the social sciences by Friedrich Schleiermacher and Wilhelm Dilthey. Dilthey argued that hermeneutics was not simply a method of understanding that was limited to particular kinds of texts, but rather that its methods could also be applied to understanding human life and behavior generally. In this way, he claimed that hermeneutics provides a systematic counterpart to the empirical explanations of the natural sciences.[10]

The starting point for contemporary hermeneutics is the claim that any exegesis of texts and, more generally, any understanding of human life and culture is both indirect and incomplete because of the kind of relationship that exists between what is to be interpreted and the interpreter (for example, experience and experiencer, text and reader, life and narrator, data and scientist). In short, like analytic philosophers, hermeneutic thinkers reject Husserl's early idea that there can be a pure description of direct experience. Like the former, hermeneutic philosophers see a gap between experience and the capturing of experience in language.

However, unlike analytic thinkers, hermeneutic philosophers view language as thoroughly historicized. For any given understanding of experience, the relationship between the data to be interpreted and the interpretation is described as circular because any given explanation of a situation presupposes certain information and knowledge, ensuring that the data subsequently included for the purposes of the enquiry is already theory-laden. In other words, each interpretation draws on specific features of the world whose salience is dependent on the background set of assumptions and possibilities of that particular interpretation. There is no uninterpreted world or life, experience or text on the one hand, and various, sometimes conflicting interpretations, on the other. What prevails are various interpretations that are grounded in earlier and other interpretations of the world.[11] Applied to scientific explanations of the world, such as Dennett's, this would mean that when scientists elect to study any given phenomenon such as subjective experience what matters about such experience is a function of a value judgment without which they would be unable to formulate even a general view about human existence. Scientific criteria do not help them make these judgments. Instead, they are based on intersubjective cultural frameworks of meaning that are prior to scientific understandings.

Martin Heidegger, who was taught by Husserl but also influenced by Dilthey and exposed to textual exegesis as a theology student, combines phenomenology and hermeneutics and comes up with a new approach to knowledge. To begin with, Heidegger accepts the hermeneutic approach to understanding the world and casts language as an activity of disclosure; rather than discovery on the one hand and distortion on the other. Take a familiar Heideggerian example: the common or garden hammer. Any claim that is made about a hammer, such as "the hammer is heavy," frames the way in which the hammer is to be viewed and considered by an observer, bringing it to light in a certain way. In this case, the truth conditions of the claim "the hammer is heavy" are satisfied on the basis of the evidence of scales or the dropping of the hammer on the foot of the unwary skeptic. What is important, however, for the purposes of a full understanding of the hammer as a phenomenon of experience, is not simply the truth or falsity of claims made about it, but the way in which language, in structuring those very claims, posits it as an object with properties. It is posited as a "thing" with properties (such as heaviness); it is an object before one's gaze. However, that the hammer is some kind of object with properties is, for Heidegger, not *the* mind-independent reality of the hammer. This is a particular reality of the hammer, as it is made available to an experiencing subject by the language deployed to describe it. The point is that, in principle, language may offer up other possible ways of experiencing the hammer—for instance, as an extension of one's hand and will in the world or, more practically, as a tool with which to mend a table.[12]

Second, Heidegger adds to this view the basic insight of phenomenology regarding the significance of the subjective perspective in any understanding of the world. The epistemological task of measuring the truth or falsity of claims in relation to a pre-existing universe is transformed for Heidegger to a task of interpretation—specifically, the task of probing the being who performs the task of interpretation.[13] This Heidegger calls *Dasein*, which he characterizes as an entity that "in its very Being, comports itself understandingly toward that Being." In other words, to understand existence is to understand the being whose *modus operandi* it is to seek this very understanding.[14] This is rather like Husserl's turn from the view that reality is mind-independent to the view that the Transcendental Ego is a condition of the world. However, the Heideggerian graft of phenomenology and hermeneutics means that a key task of interpretation is the task of interpreting the situation of interpretation as opposed to mapping out the structures of the Transcendental Ego via the *epoché*. Heidegger is concerned here to replace both the Cartesian notion of the *cogito* and the Husserlian notion of the Ego with the notion of *Dasein*. This is because he views both the Cogito and the Ego as representing human subjectivity as an unproblematic perspective that measures phenomena against neutral criteria; whether these are the neutral criteria of science or of phenomenology is no matter. His alternative account posits the human subject as interpreter of meaning and as already in the world, chastened by his situatedness in a body, language, history, and culture.

THE DETOUR OF INTERPRETATION

Ricoeur claims that his account of the self is, on the one hand, an advance from Cartesian and Husserlian privileging of the subject and, on the other, a way of unraveling the hermeneutic emphasis on the embodied and historical situatedness of such a subject. In sum, Ricoeur, like Heidegger, grafts hermeneutics and phenomenology in his analysis of the subject, but, unlike Heidegger, Ricoeur's graft ends in *detour* rather than *Dasein*. I will explain.

First of all, Ricoeur argues that a "realist theory of meaning" (the rough equivalent of the realist thesis I sketched in chapter 3) must address the skeptic's worry that the relationship between mental states and real world events can never be probed from any external position:

> Does not one grant oneself, in a realist theory of meaning, the very thing whose origin one is seeking in the variations inscribed within the real situation? By ascribing the variation to the description of events and not to that of mental states, to be sure, one protects oneself from subjectivism and psychologism, but one does not escape the linguistic framework of description. . . . What is a situation that is not already interpreted, even if this be only in the categorizing of properties and relations?. . . [F]rom what external position does one perceive the correspondence between the mental situation and the factual situation?[15]

Echoing Heidegger, he argues that the world and the self are knowable only through the detour of interpretation. He deploys the term "detour" to flag his belief that the operation of interpretation does not access the world directly.[16] His point is that the objects of nature and culture along with subjective access to them are not immediately known, nor is there a value-free or neutral language through which they can be transparently rendered.

> What the phenomenologist objects to is the primacy assigned to the environment, which the experimentalist considers as a world wholly made up of things from which messages emanate and to which replies are given. . . . The human agent does not content him-

self with being informed about his environment in order possibly to modify it afterward; from the beginning he interprets it and shapes it, or better—to use Husserl's strong formulation, in the last unpublished writings—he constitutes it as the world that surrounds him by projecting onto it the aims of his action and his demands for meaning.... What really has to be considered is the pragmatic constitution of what Husserl called the life-world (*Lebenswelt*) rather than the projections of the brain upon a world supposed already to have been organized.[17]

What is disclosed about the world at any given time, for Ricoeur, (including what is disclosed by scientific frameworks) are various interpretations that are culturally, historically, and socially mediated. In his "Intellectual Autobiography" he describes his project in the following way: "I distanced myself from a self-consciousness that would be immediate, direct, and transparent to itself, and pleaded instead for the necessity of a detour by the signs and the works displayed in the cultural world."[18]

Ricoeur distinguishes his position from Heidegger's, however, because he is concerned with the specter of irrealism that he claims haunts the Heideggerian stance. He identifies two central problems with the Heideggerian solution: (1) that it is not clear how a historical understanding can be derived from Heidegger's emphasis on the return to the origins of interpretation (in *Dasein*), and (2) that it does not provide a method of evaluating between conflicting rival interpretations. Ricoeur describes the problem with Heidegger's move from epistemological to ontological considerations as one that might lead to the construction of a closed system, one incapable of being critiqued from within or without:

> With Heidegger's philosophy, we are always engaged in going back to the foundations, but we are left incapable of beginning the movement of return, which would lead from the fundamental ontology to the properly epistemological question of the status of the human sciences. Now a philosophy which breaks the dialogue with the sciences is no longer addressed to anything but itself. . . . For me, the question which remains unresolved in Heidegger's work is this: how can a question of critique in general be accounted for within the framework of a fundamental hermeneutics?[19]

In this, Ricoeur is like Dennett who, as we saw in chapter 1, had similar fears about Rorty's position. Ricoeur's fear is that the hermeneutic approach provides no means, independent or otherwise, of evaluating any of its claims about the world. He frames the question that the hermeneutic philosopher must answer in the following terms: "[I]n expressing itself, how can life objectify itself, and, in objectifying itself, how does it bring to light meanings capable of being taken up and understood by another historical being, who overcomes his own historical situation?"[20] What is clear from Ricoeur's objections to Heidegger's metaphysics is that he, Ricoeur, is concerned to show that a commitment to an interpretative model of explanation provides a means of deciding between rival interpretations, and that meaning can somehow be "brought to light" and communicated across cultural and historical divides.

The strategy that Ricoeur employs to achieve this is to argue that the detour of interpretation is constrained by the basic conditions mentioned in the introduction to this chapter, namely reflexivity, intentionality, corporeality, temporality, and intersubjectivity. Granted these boundary conditions, any given interpretation—for example, any account of the self—is restricted accordingly. So, even if there is interpretation going on, the outcome is not arbitrary. On the contrary, for Ricoeur, an adequate account of any given phenomenon (the self in this case) should incorporate these features of human existence. Moreover, conflicting accounts of the self can be tested on the degree to which they successfully reflect them. In order to get a sense of what Ricoeur is trying to do, I will look at the condition of reflexivity and its relationship to an understanding of the self in a little more detail.

REFLEXIVITY

Like Husserl, Ricoeur identifies with, but also distinguishes his position from, the Cartesian approach to thinking about the self, which he calls "reflexive philosophy."[21] This is

> the mode of thought stemming from the Cartesian *cogito* and handed down by way of Kant and French post-Kantian philosophy. . . . A reflexive philosophy considers the most radical philosophical problems to be those which concern the possibility of self-understanding as the subject of the operations of knowing, willing, evaluating, etc.[22]

For Ricoeur, what is fundamental and correct about this kind of philosophical approach is its privileging of reflexive *activities* such as speaking, willing, and evaluating as a means of self-knowledge. However, what is equally fundamental and erroneous, for him, is the twofold way in which this position has traditionally responded to its privileging. First, it has concluded that such activities, of themselves, warrant elevation to modes of knowledge of the self. Second, it has elevated the self, thus known, to the status of a "thing" with moral properties. Ricoeur notes that the "*I*" of reflexive activities such as "*I* think" or "*I* doubt" is indeed perceived; it is "felt" with certainty, but not in a way that yields genuine knowledge of the self. The very incorrigibility of the *cogito* means that it cannot tell anything about any genuine features of the self. He puts it in the following way:

> No doubt I have an apperception of myself and my acts, and this apperception is a type of evidence. Descartes cannot be dislodged from this incontestable proposition: I cannot doubt myself without perceiving that I doubt. But what does this apperception signify? A certitude, certainly, but a certitude devoid of truth. As Malebranche well understood, in opposition to Descartes, this immediate grasp is only a feeling and not an idea. . . . I only sense that I exist and that I think; I sense that I am awake; such is apperception.[23]

Comparisons can be drawn between this Husserlian inspired objection to the Cartesian treatment of reflexivity and Dennett's rejection of the Cartesian account of consciousness sketched in chapter 1 above. There I outlined Dennett's thesis that the capacity for human consciousness had traditionally led philosophers to conclude that wherever there was a conscious mind, there was a point of view or observer who took in a limited amount of the available information on any given space-time continuum. For Dennett, the unwarranted move was made when theorists, such as Descartes, attempted to describe and locate such a point of view within the individual. On Dennett's account, difficulties with description and location prompted the Cartesian conclusion that the possibility of having conscious thoughts, or a point of view, implies that these are properties of a *res cogitans* or thinking thing: a real self. Having set out the moves involved in Cartesian dualism, Dennett rejected it because it ultimately failed to explain the operations of consciousness and placed the subject of consciousness at a further remove.

Adopting a similar strategy to Dennett, but one that accepts Husserl's phenomenological step back, Ricoeur understands the activity of reflexion in a way which distinguishes his account of the self from the largely solipsistic Cartesian *cogito*, but also from the Husserlian Transcendental Ego, and indeed, though it is not explicitly stated, from a Dennettian theorist's fiction. In short, for Ricoeur, what is significant about reflexive activities or operations is not their supposed direct access to the self:

> "To say self is not to say *I*. The *I* is posited—or is deposed. The *self* is implied reflexively in the operations, the analysis of which precedes the return toward this self."[24]

First of all, he refers to Cartesian and anti-Cartesian accounts as deploying reflexivity in order to pronounce or denounce the self. He claims that the "*I*" is posited or deposed: the first-person pronoun is postulated as either real (by, for example, Descartes) or fictional (by, for example, Hume). Alternatively, his claim is that the self is "*implied* reflexively"; in other words, the self, understood as a unified or continuous entity, is not *prior* to the operations of reflexion, but rather, it is *engendered* by them. In this, Ricoeur's position is close to Dennett's, whose argument, as outlined in chapter 1, is that the self does not exist prior to consciousness, but rather that it is the product of the operations of consciousness. For Ricoeur, it is because human beings have the capacity to speak, act, tell stories, and evaluate that it is possible to count them as selves. Specifically, for example, it is in the telling of stories over time that a particular self becomes recognizable as having a gender or profession, belonging to a family and place. Moreover, because these stories are culturally, socially, and historically mediated, the self that they imply is also mediated: "[T]he self does not know itself immediately, but only indirectly, through the detour of cultural signs of all sorts, which articulate the self in symbolic mediations that already articulate action."[25]

What is innovative about Ricoeur's understanding of reflexivity is that it conjoins two very different processes: the activities of the concrete human being (speaking, acting, etc.) as well as the operation of cultural mediation that is involved in any interpretative task. Ricoeur manages to remain within the tradition of reflexive philosophy while radically transforming it.[26]

The self, conceived on the basis of his new under-standing of reflexivity, is neither immediately nor trans-parently known. It is known via available discourses, which may include the discourses of history, literature, and psychology as well as the naturalist discourses of neuroscience, cognitive psychology, and biology. Impor-tantly, the latter are not privileged over the former.

THE PROBLEM OF PERSONAL IDENTITY

Granted his new understanding of the self, Ricoeur takes on the task of resolving the traditional problem of per-sonal identity—the problem of establishing the condi-tions of the identity of the self through time. He views the problem of personal identity as originating, in part, in confusion about what it takes for human beings, as opposed to objects in general, to persist in time—what it takes to obey what he calls "the principle of permanence in time."[27] This requirement traditionally entails that in order for any person at time T2 to be deemed identical with any person at time T1, the former would have to share some significant features with the latter—some set of features would have to endure through the passage of time. Something about the person at T2 would have had to remain the *same*. Analyzing the concept of sameness, Ricoeur points to a number of ways in which analytic theories have attempted to delineate it. He notes that the concept of sameness is paradigmatically defined as a rela-tion of *numerical identity*, a relation between two or more occurrences of one and the same object (for example, one room described at different times). The uniqueness of a thing is what is significant here. A second and less strict account of sameness posits it as a relation of *qualitative identity* where strong resemblances between items mean that they can be substituted for one another without serious import (for example, two sandwiches, both made from cheddar cheese and white bread). While numerical and qualitative senses of identity are very different, Ricoeur draws attention to the way in which they are related. This is due to the passage and the ravages of time:

> [I]t is precisely to the extent that time is implied in the series of occurrences of the same thing that the reidentification of the same can provoke hesitation, doubt, or contestation; the extreme resemblance between two or more occurrences can then be invoked as an indirect criterion to reinforce the presumption of numerical identity. This is what happens when we speak of the physical identity of a person. We have no trouble recognizing someone who simply enters and leaves, appears, disappears and reappears. Yet doubt is not far away when we compare a present perception with a recent memory. . . . Hence a defendant appearing in court may object that he is not the same as the one who was incriminated. What happens then? One compares the individual present to the material marks held to be the irrecusable traces of his earlier presence in the very places at issue. It happens that this comparison is extended to eyewitness accounts, which, with a much greater margin of uncertainty, are held to be equivalent to the past presenta-

tion of the individual examined. . . . The trials of war
criminals have occasioned just such confrontations
along with, as we know, the ensuing risks and uncertainties.[28]

It is because of the passage of time and the uncertainties
it brings that qualitative sameness can act to reassure us
with regard to quantitative sameness. Nevertheless,
doubts can remain as to whether or not the person identified at T2 is actually the same person identified at T1. To
address these doubts, a third aspect of the notion of identity is invoked. This is the notion of *uninterrupted continuity*: that the identity of trees or animals or the human
species (as opposed to persons) is assured if their
growth or aging process can be mapped or pho-
tographed as a series of small changes which "taken one
by one, threaten resemblance without destroying it."[29]
Both qualitative identity and the notion of uninterrupted
continuity, then, provide some kind of evidence for the
persistence of numerical identity. Even so, the ravages of
time remain a constant threat to the conviction that one
and the same entity persists.

In this regard, Ricoeur argues in favor of the Kantian
solution to the threat of time, which is to posit some kind
of structure, organization, or system that persists over the
course of time and change. Rather than relying on a
Cartesian immutable substance or substrate, Kant's innovation was to conceive of substance as a relation or principle. While Descartes viewed substance as some kind of
permanent matter underlying an object of perception
and enduring while perceptions of that object changed,

Kant deployed the notion of substance in a way that no longer referred it to an object. Instead, he deployed it as a relational category to describe whatever features of objects—structural or organizational—that endure through change. In the "First Analogy of Experience" in the *Critique of Pure Reason* Kant posits substance as the "permanence of the real in time, that is, the representation of the real as a substrate of empirical determination to time in general, and so as abiding while all else changes."[30] Ricoeur describes this Kantian move as a strengthening of the notion that changes can occur to an entity that is conceived as not changing:

> This is why the threat it [time] represents for identity is not entirely dissipated unless we can posit, at the base of similitude and of the uninterrupted continuity, a principle of *permanence in time*. This will be, for example, the invariable structure of a tool, all of whose parts will gradually have been replaced. This is also the case, of supreme interest to us, of the permanence of the genetic code of a biologic individual; what remains here is the organization of a combinatory system. The idea of structure, opposed to that of event, replies to this criterion of identity, the strongest one that can be applied. It confirms the relational character of identity, which does not appear in the ancient formulation of substance but which Kant reestablishes by classifying substance among the categories of relation, as the condition of the possibility of conceiving of change as happening to something which does not change, at least not in the moment of attributing the accident to the substance; permanence

in time thus becomes the transcendental of numerical identity. The entire problematic of personal identity will revolve around this search for a relational invariant, giving it the strong signification of permanence in time.[31]

The task that Kantian theorists of identity must address is the delineation of such a "relational invariant" that will meet the principle of permanence in time. Such an invariant might be posited as the structure or organization of an entity—for example, the biological structure of an individual. This can be said to endure even while the components or parts are changed or replaced. Ricoeur calls this relation of identity a relation of *sameness* or *idem*-identity (Latin *idem*, German *Gleichheit,* French *mêmeté*).[32] Applied to persons on a biological level, it invokes features like the permanence and uniqueness of organismic morphologies and finger-prints, and, on a psychological level, it invokes sameness of character and dispositions.

What distinguishes Ricoeur from the Kantian solution, however, is that Ricoeur pays attention to a second sense of self that he claims is implicit in the Kantian account but which captures what distinguishes human beings from other kinds of objects.

Does the selfhood of the self imply a form of permanence in time which is not reducible to the determination of a substratum, not even in the relational sense which Kant assigns to the category of substance; in short, is there a form of permanence in time which is not simply the schema of the category of substance?

> . . . Is there a form of permanence in time which can
> be connected to the question "who?" inasmuch as it is
> irreducible to any question of "what?" Is there a form
> of permanence in time that is a reply to the question
> "Who am I?"[33]

Following Heidegger, Ricoeur's solution to the
problem—"Is there a form of permanence in time that is
a reply to the question 'Who am I?'"—is to view the continuity of the self through time in terms of a second relation of identity, which he calls a relation of *selfhood* or
ipse-identity (Latin *ipse*, German *Selbstheit*, French
ipséité).[34] *Idem*-identity is, paradigmatically, the sameness of objects; *ipse*-identity is, paradigmatically, the selfhood of reflexive beings. Ricoeur notes that although the
two relations of identity—*idem* and *ipse*—are very different; they intersect to the extent that they both display
features that endure through time, and they both display
temporal continuity. Taking the concept of "character,"
Ricoeur acknowledges that he had originally posited it in
*Freedom and Nature: The Voluntary and the Involun-
tary* as capturing a set of distinctive features about an
individual that could just as well be described from a
third-person point of view. As such, the notion of character was perceived as a good candidate for the identification and reidentification of the human individual over
time. It qualified as an *idem*-identity, as that which
remained the same about a person even through the passage of time and change: "As an absolute involuntary, I
assigned it, along with the unconscious and with being
alive, symbolized by birth, to that level of our existence

which we cannot change but to which we must consent."[35] The immutable nature of character was again reiterated in *Fallible Man*, this time as it might be experienced from the first person point of view, as a "finite perspective affecting my opening to the world of things, ideas, values, and persons."[36]

With *Oneself as Another*, however, Ricoeur widens the notion of character to express a more dynamic dimension than he had attributed to it in the past. He describes character as "the set of lasting dispositions by which a person is recognized" and views dispositions in terms of two other notions: *habits* and *acquired identifications*. First, a habit, according to Ricoeur, has a twofold meaning and refers to what is already acquired and, also, what is in the process of being formed: "habit gives a history to character, but this is a history in which sedimentation tends to cover the innovation which preceded it, even to the point of abolishing the latter."[37] So, a habit is not always static but involves a "dialectic of innovation and sedimentation."[38] By this, he means that any personal habit is initially acquired through a dynamic activity even if it is eventually cast as a distinguishing mark by which a person is recognized and reidentified.

Second, Ricoeur views a disposition as an "acquired identification" with some set of values, ideals, or role models.[39] Again, in this case, the process of identification is, in part, a dynamic and evaluative activity, where the recognition of norms or heroes, in turn, contributes to the subsequent molding of oneself in terms of them. This is what Ricoeur calls the "dialectic of otherness and internalization."[40] On the one hand, what he can conclude of his conceptualization of character is that it "assures at once numerical identity, qualitative identity, uninterrupted continuity across change, and, finally, permanence in time which defines sameness" or *idem*-identity.[41] On the other hand, both the dialectic of innovation and sedimentation and the dialectic of otherness and internalization serve to draw attention to the unstable and evaluative origins of character that for Ricoeur "remind us that character has a history which it has contracted."[42] And so, the sense of self as character with *idem*-identity is enriched and energized by a sense of self as contractor with *ipse*-identity. This also captures the experience of many people who describe their sense of time in two different ways. On the one hand, they consider that their basic character perseveres over time. On the other, they focus on their faithfulness over time to the promises they make (think of the many uses of the term "contract" in western societies). (Ricoeur conjoins the notion of self with the notion of character in yet another innovative fashion—as a character in a play or novel—which is discussed in chapter 6.)

The relation of *ipse*-identity finds its fullest expression in the notion of *self-constancy*. The latter relation provides the idea of a self that can be recognized and reidentified over time but is not, itself, a real unchanging core:

> Keeping one's word expresses a self-constancy which cannot be inscribed, as character was, within the dimension of something in general but solely within the dimension of "who?" Here, too, common usage is a

good guide. The perseverance of character is one thing; the perseverance of faithfulness to a word that has been given is something else again. The continuity of character is one thing, the constancy of friendship is quite another.[43]

Ricoeur distinguishes here between the constancy of character—dispositional traits, habits, identifications—and the constancy of a bond—keeping one's word, remaining faithful, even in the face of radical changes of character:[44] "[T]he paradigm of *ipse* identity is, for me, making a promise. I shall hold firm, even if I change; it is an identity that is willed, sustained, one that proclaims itself despite change."[45]

This distinction between the constancy of character and bond raises the objection that the constancy one keeps to a bond must ultimately rely on the constancy of one's character. Think, for example, of a person who commits herself to a monogamous relationship with another. It could be argued that she is less likely to succeed in her commitment if she goes through a radical personality or lifestyle change, or, indeed, simply meets someone else whom she finds more desirable. In this case, the constancy of bond is dependent on the constancy of character. The two relations of identity, *idem* and *ipse*, cannot be peeled apart; the latter is parasitic on and reducible to the former.

However, Ricoeur might try to refute this objection because he defines *ipse* in the following terms: "[E]ven if my desire were to change, even if I were to change my opinion or my inclination, 'I will hold firm.'"[46] Returning to the example, it could be argued that the continued maintenance of hollow or brutal marriages in the light of certain religious beliefs is strong evidence in favor of the thesis that a human being can view her self as holding firm in spite of changes in circumstances and character. Even so, there is no need for such an extreme example. What is at stake here, and what, on any adequate account must be rendered, is the sense we have about any issue at all—trivial or fundamental—that we can initiate or terminate, participate or withdraw from our commitments, even if they are dependant on our character and dispositions. Should theorists from neuroscience, cognitive psychology, sociobiology, and genetics all confirm, for example, that I have a particular kind of nature with specific traits and characteristics, they do not fully answer the questions "who am I?" and "what will I do?" from a Ricoeurian perspective. In this way, Ricoeur drives a wedge between objectifying accounts of the self, on the one hand, and his account of a self as somehow capable of resisting its reduction to naturalist descriptions.

THE NUMBER OF SELVES, IDENTITY RELATIONS, AND TESTS OF TRUTH

Ricoeur argues that there is a "profound structural difference" between the identity relations of *ipse* and *idem* and describes as a "working hypothesis" the idea that "the distinction between selfhood and sameness does not simply concern two constellations of meaning but involves two modes of being."[47] He also claims that the two relations of identity are distinguishable logically, epistemologically, and ontologically: "I want to emphasize the break which separates *idem* [sameness] and *ipse* [selfhood] as being not only grammatical, or even epistemological and logical but really ontological."[48] This calls for a detailed analysis.

Ricoeur claims that, first, the relation of identity as sameness is logically distinct from the relation of identity as selfhood. This means that the conditions that have to be met by a person at T2 in order to be considered *idem*-identical with a person at T1 are not equivalent to the conditions that have to be met by a person at T2 in order to be considered *ipse*-identical with a person at T1. For example, as discussed, a condition of *idem*-identity might be the continuity of a person's character over time, while a condition of *ipse*-identity might be the continuity of a person's bond.

Second, Ricoeur's claim that the two relations are ontologically distinct implies that these relations do not have the same referent. Indeed, on my reading of Ricoeur, the self whose continuity is based on *ipse*-identity does not seem to be the sort of thing that has a clear referent at all. I take from Ricoeur's claim about the ontological status of the different identity relations that the *idem* relation refers to the continuity of features of a human being such as character, dispositions, or brain/body continuity, while the *ipse* relation refers to particular sets of activities of a human being which take time such as developing long-term projects, making commitments, or claiming ownership of one's thoughts or one's body.

Third, Ricoeur claims that the relation of identity as sameness is epistemologically distinct from the relation of identity as selfhood. This means that the two relations of identity are verified in accordance with two different forms of assessment. *Idem*-identity can be verified by Cartesian certainty or objective criteria (for example, taking fingerprints), while *ipse*-identity is verified by what he calls "attestation." The latter is an epistemological standard of truth that is critical to Ricoeur's account of the self and it is examined and assessed in chapter 5.

Granted the distinction between the relations of *idem* and *ipse*, at least two kinds of self are possible: the thing-like real self with its *idem* identity conditions and the unity of action, or capable self, with its *ipse* identity conditions. Importantly, these two selves should not be construed as two aspects of a more basic self—Ricoeur's account of the self is not dualist. Instead, both the real and the capable self can be construed as unities that are the outcome of distinct interpretative detours. What emerges is an argument of the following sort:

- The world and its phenomena are revealed to us through interpretation.
- Interpretation is constrained by basic or boundary conditions of human existence such as temporality and corporeality.
- The concept of self is delineated through interpretation and is therefore mediated via the constraints of the boundary conditions.
- Different frameworks for interpreting the self are

possible (e.g., the frameworks of science and phenomenological hermeneutics).

- Different accounts of the self emerge from these different frameworks, e.g., the self as real and the self as capable.
- These accounts of the self are not reducible to one another; they are configured as "two modes of being."[49]

To conclude, Ricoeur's graft of hermeneutics and phenomenology must be welcomed because it advances the debate about the self beyond the idea that it is either real or illusory. The ultimate success of Ricoeur's position, however, does not rest solely on his negative criticisms of traditional solutions to the problem of the self and its identity. Ricoeur, like Dennett, holds the view that selves are not real in the Cartesian sense and opts for a more fragile variety. However, as I argued in earlier chapters, Dennett's concept of the self turned out to be at best fragile and fictional, and at worst irrelevant. Alternatively, Ricoeur's account proposes the idea of a capable self, stabilized because it is grounded in activities and constrained by the human condition. What remains to be established is the degree to which the model of the capable self does more theoretical and practical work than the alternatives. Given what we have learned about Ricoeur's grafting of phenomenology and hermeneutics, it could be argued that his account of the capable self is theoretically more foundational than the Cartesian account of the real self or Dennett's account of the fictional self because it incorporates the boundary conditions of human existence in a way that the others do not. I will return to this later. First of all, the particular way in which the identity of the capable self is determined or attested must be evaluated if we are to take his account of the self seriously. This will be the task of the following chapters.

NOTES TO CHAPTER 4

1. In *Time and Narrative* 3 (*TN3*), Ricoeur suggests that the identity of both individuals and communities can be conceived as a narrative (*TN3*, trans. Kathleen Blamey and David Pellauer [Chicago: University of Chicago Press, 1988], p. 247. It was originally published as *Temps et Récit* 3 [Paris: Editions du Seuil, 1983]). In *TN3*, the outlines of a narrative account of identity were only sketchily drawn. However, when invited to deliver the Gifford Lectures in Edinburgh in 1986, Ricoeur purposed to consider the implications of his claim for individual identity. His lectures in Edinburgh formed the basis of *Soi-même comme un autre* (Paris: Editions du Seuil, 1990), translated as *Oneself as Another*, trans. Kathleen Blamey (Chicago: University of Chicago Press, 1992). See also Paul Ricoeur, "From Psychoanalysis to the Question of the Self, or Thirty Years of Philosophical Work," in *Critique and Conviction: Conversation with François Azouvi and Marc de Launay*, trans. Kathleen Blamey (Cambridge: Polity Press, 1998), pp. 68–94; Paul Ricoeur, "Memory and Forgetting," in *Questioning Ethics*, ed. Richard Kearney and Mark Dooley (London: Routledge, 1999), pp. 5–11; Paul Ricoeur, "Imagination, Testimony and Trust, A dialogue with Paul Ricoeur," in ibid., pp. 12–17; and Paul Ricoeur, *The Just*, p. 1–10.

2. More detail will follow, but briefly, the notion of reflex-

ivity describes self-awareness and self-understanding; corporeality places emphasis on one's embodiment and affective as well as intellectual access to the world; intentionality captures the way in which human consciousness is in a relationship with the world; temporality acknowledges that human beings have a specific relationship with time; and, finally, intersubjectivity refers to the way in which human selves are socially constructed.

3. I discuss the concept of the capable self in greater detail in chapter 5.

4. My focus in this book is on the narrative identity of the capable self, even though Ricoeur also argues that the capable self is unified through speech, action, and moral agency. See, for example, Ricoeur, *Oneself as Another*, studies 7, 8, and 9 for a further elaboration of his account of moral agency.

5. Paul Ricoeur, "Intellectual Autobiography," in *Philosophy of Paul Ricoeur*, ed. Lewis Edwin Hahn (Chicago and La Salle, Illinois: Open Court, 1995), p. 16. In his "Intellectual Biography," Ricoeur acknowledges his debt to both phenomenological and hermeneutic thinkers (for example, Edmund Husserl, Martin Heidegger, Maurice Merleau-Ponty, Hans-Georg Gadamer, and Roland Barthes).

6. For example, the central claim of Wittgenstein in *Tractatus Logico-Philosophicus*, trans. D. F. Pears and B. F. McGuinness (London: Routledge, 1961) is that true propositions are like pictures of facts (not objects). Therefore, he shifts his attention away from the ontological status of objects and toward an investigation of grammatical rules and linguistic practices.

It is important to point out that the constitutive role of language in the production of meaning is also explored in other traditions and disciplines—in addition to Wittgenstein in analytic philosophy, other important figures include Gottlob Frege, J. L. Austin, and John Searle; in linguistics there is Ferdinand de Saussure; in psychoanalysis are Jacques Lacan and Luce Irigaray; and in literary theory are Jacques Derrida and Julia Kristeva.

7. It is associated with the messenger god, Hermes, who was credited with the discovery of language and writing. For a helpful summary of the historical background to hermeneutics, see Richard E. Palmer, *Hermeneutics* (Evanston: Northwestern University Press, 1969). See also Ricoeur's two essays "Existence and Hermeneutics," in *The Conflict of Interpretations*, ed. Don Ihde, trans. Kathleen Blamey (Evanston: Northwestern University Press, 1974), pp. 3–24 and "The Task of Hermeneutics," in *Hermeneutics and the Human Sciences*, ed. and trans. John B. Thompson (Cambridge: Cambridge University Press, 1981), pp. 43–62.

8. Aristotle, *De Interpretatione* in *The Complete Works of Aristotle* 1, ed. Jonathan Barnes, Bollingen Series LXXI (Princeton, NJ: Princeton University Press, 1984), pp. 25–38.

9. Cited in Palmer, *Hermeneutics*, p. 34.

10. Wilhelm Dilthey, "The Rise of Hermeneutics," *New Literary History* 3, no. 2 (Winter 1972): 229–244.

11. Heidegger later insisted that what is known as the "hermeneutic circle" is not a vicious kind of circularity. There is circularity involved because the hermeneutic claim is that any enquiry is governed by presumptions that dictate its outcome and Heidegger acknowledges this:

> Is there not, however, a manifest circularity in such an undertaking? If we must first define an entity *in its Being*, and if we want to formulate the question of Being only on this basis, what is this but going in a circle? In working out our question, have we not "presupposed" something which only the answer can

bring? (*Being and Time*, trans. John Macquarrie and Edward Robinson [Oxford: Blackwell, 1973], H 7)

But Heidegger also claims that the circularity is not closed because the enquiry itself frames the phenomena in a particular way that both sets the parameters of the outcome of the enquiry and also elicits further questions and further frames which enhance our understanding. That the mode of enquiry itself is implicated in knowledge leads Heidegger to turn his attention to the situation of the enquirer. (Note my references to Heidegger's *Being and Time*, such as H 7 above, indicate the pagination of the later German editions which is printed on the margins of the 1973 publication.)

12. Heidegger, *Being and Time*, H 69, 78, 83, 109, 154, 157, 360.

13. Ricoeur describes this as a reversal of the usual epistemological question. For him, instead of asking, "On what condition can a knowing subject understand a text or history?" one asks, "What kind of being is it whose being consists of understanding?" (Ricoeur, "Existence and Hermeneutics," p. 6)

14. Heidegger, *Being and Time*, H 78, part one, section II, number 12.

15. Ricoeur "Reply to Dabney Townsend," in *The Philosophy of Paul Ricoeur*, ed. Lewis Edwin Hahn (Chicago and La Salle, Illinois: Open Court, 1995), p. 212.

16. Ricoeur, *OA*, p. 297.

17. Ricoeur in Jean-Pierre Changeux and Paul Ricoeur, *What Makes Us Think?* (Princeton: Princeton University Press, 2000), p. 89–90.

18. Ricoeur, "Intellectual Autobiography," p. 19. Ricoeur describes the operation of hermeneutic analysis as involving a detour of a particular kind, an "indirect approach of reflection through the detour of analysis" (Ricoeur, *OA*, p. 297).

19. Ricoeur, "The Task of Hermeneutics," p. 59.

20. Ricoeur, "Existence and Hermeneutics," p. 5.

21. In the ordinary meaning of reflexivity, an activity—for example, Joan shooting herself in the foot—is considered reflexive because the subject and the object of the shooting are the same individual. Clearly, a great number of philosophers including those that concern us here have greatly added to this basic sense of reflexivity.

22. Paul Ricoeur, "On Interpretation," in *Philosophy in France Today*, ed. A. Montefiore (Cambridge: Cambridge University Press, 1983), p. 188.

23. Paul Ricoeur, *Freud and Philosophy: An Essay on Interpretation*, trans. Denis Savage (New Haven: Yale University Press, 1970), p. 44.

24. Ricoeur, *OA*, p. 18.

25. Paul Ricoeur, "Narrative Identity," *Philosophy Today* (Spring 1991): 80.

26. The refinement of the term *réflexive* by Ricoeur's translator, Kathleen Blamey, gives force to Ricoeur's deployment of it as emphasizing the difference between his account and Cartesian alternatives. Blamey explains that the French term *réflexive* lends itself to two possible English translations. It has both a *reflexive* aspect, meaning self-referring, and a *reflective* aspect, meaning mediated:

"[R]eflexive philosophy"... is a subject-oriented philosophy, reflexive in the subject's act of turning back upon itself, analogous to the grammatical sense, and as "reflective philosophy" in the more general sense of contemplation, mediation, but including as well the reference to self-reference. Since the French term embraces both reflexive/reflective, the choice of one or the other in English should allow the resonance of the term excluded to be heard (Kathleen Blamey, "From the Ego to the Self: A Philosophical Itinerary," in *The Philosophy of Paul Ricoeur*, ed. Lewis Edwin Hahn, p. 602, fn. 37).

27. Ricoeur, *OA*, pp. 116–117.

28. Ibid.

29. Ibid., p. 117.

30. Immanuel Kant, *Critique of Pure Reason*, trans. Norman Kemp Smith (New York: St. Martin's Press, 1995), p. 184; cited in Ricoeur, "Narrative Identity," p. 74.

31. Ricoeur, *OA*, pp. 117–118.

32. Ibid., p. 116.

33. Ibid., p. 118.

34. Ibid., p. 116. See also *OA*, p. 309; fn.11 points to a close kinship between Ricoeur's notion of *ipse*-identity and Heidegger's notions of *Vorhandenheit* (presence-at-hand) and *Selbst-Ständigkeit* (self-constancy). The important move that Ricoeur makes with regard to Heideggerian questions regarding the self is to apply them to the problem of personal identity as it has evolved in the analytic tradition. Having said that, it is instructive to recall the way in which Heidegger first outlined the relationship between the self and time in *Being and Time*:

> What seems "simpler" than to characterize the "connectedness of life" between birth and death? It consists of a sequence of Experiences "in time."... In spite of the constant changing of these Experiences, the Self maintains itself throughout with a certain self-sameness. Opinions diverge as to how that which thus persists is to be defined, and how one is to determine what relation it may possibly have to the changing Experiences. The Being of this perversely changing connectedness of Experiences remains indefinite. But

at bottom, whether one likes it or not, in this way of characterizing the connectedness of life, one has posited something present-at-hand "in time," something that is obviously "un-Thinglike." . . . With the analysis of the specific movement and persistence which belong to Dasein's historizing, we come back to . . . the question of the constancy of the Self, which we defined as the "who" of Dasein. Self-constancy is a way of Being of Dasein, and is therefore grounded in a specific temporalizing of temporality (Heidegger, *Being and Time*, H 373, 374, 375).

35. Ricoeur, *OA*, p. 119.

36. Ibid., p. 120.

37. Ibid., p. 121.

38. Ibid., p. 122.

39. Ibid.

40. Ibid.

41. Ibid.

42. Ibid.

43. Ibid., p. 123.

44. Ibid., p. 118.

45. Paul Ricoeur, "From Psychoanalysis to the Question of the Self, or Thirty Years of Philosophical Work," p. 90.

46. Ricoeur, *OA*, p. 124.

47. Ibid., p. 309. Elsewhere, Ricoeur calls *ipse* and *idem* "two figures of identity" (Ricoeur, "From Psychoanalysis to the Question of the Self, or Thirty Years of Philosophical Work," p. 90).

48. Ricoeur, "Narrative Identity," p. 75.

49. Ricoeur, *OA*, p. 309.

Chapter Five

THE CAPABLE SELF AND ITS NARRATIVE IDENTITY

The success of Ricoeur's account of the capable self depends on whether or not he can clearly determine the conditions of its *ipse*-identity. As I will show, one of the ways in which he claims that this can be done is by unifying the events of an individual's life on the basis of "emplotment" or narrative ordering. He calls this the narrative identity of the self.[1] Furthermore, he posits a set of standards against which the identity of the self can be tested. This he describes as a new order of truth: attestation. This chapter probes Ricoeur's account of the capable self, its narrative identity, and attestation.

Where Dennett seeks to retain a role for psychological language within a naturalist explanation of our sense of self which privileges the language of the brain sciences, Ricoeur radically distinguishes between both languages. At the same time, he refuses to concede that separating out brain/body talk and mind/mental talk implies that the former treats of matter and the latter of something other than matter. Arguing that "[r]eductionism is a reaction against ontological dualism," he claims that both neuroscientific and psychological languages are discourses of the body.[2]

> Mental experience implies the corporeal, but in a sense that is irreducible to the objective bodies studied by the natural sciences. Semantically opposed to the body-as-object of these sciences is the experienced body, one's own body—my body (from which I speak), your body (the body that belongs to you, which I address), the body of another (his body or her body, about which I make up stories). . . . My initial hypothesis, then, which I submit for your consideration, is that I do not see a way of passing from one order of discourse to the other: either I speak of neurons and so forth, in which case I find myself in a certain language, or I speak of thoughts, actions, and feelings that I connect with my body, to which I stand in a relation of possession, of belonging. Thus I can say that my hands, my feet, and so forth are my organs in the sense that I walk with my feet, I grasp with my hands—but this comes under the head of personal experience, I do not have to commit myself to an ontology of the soul in order to speak in this way. By contrast, when I am told that I have a brain, no actual experience corresponds to this; I learn about it in books.[3]

Granted that we can speak about our direct and personal experiences and activities in ways that neither invoke the idea of a soul substance nor rely on the objectifying discourses of the sciences, Ricoeur argues that we can reconceive of the self as a unity of action rather than as some kind of real thing. I call this self the "capable self" borrowing the term from one of his interviews where he refers to the "capable person" as the one who says "I can": "For the question of the capable person is, successively, the question of determining who can speak, who can act, who can recount, who can impute actions to himself or herself?"[4] It is also drawn from Ricoeur's idea of the "capable subject" who is able to speak, take, touch, and so on to varying degrees. In the latter case, Ricoeur defines "capacity" as an ability that is known and felt from direct experience rather than as a disposition that is attributed to human beings on the basis of neuroscientific evidence alone (and independently of first-person evidence).[5]

> The word capacity means "I am capable of," which is to say "I can do something," where I am the one who feels the availability and limits of these powers—I can take, I can touch, and so on. But the same word will have an entirely functional meaning in the vocabulary of the neurosciences that does not assume that anyone feels this capacity.[6]

Ricoeur's claim is something like the following: "I know, or I am assured, that I am a unique persisting self—an *ipse*-identity—through actions such as speaking, doing, telling stories or responding as a moral agent." Ricoeur's account of the capable self conjures a notion of the self that is neither wholly substantial nor wholly fictional. It is unique, not because it is a single object, a locatable substance in the brain or elsewhere, but because uniqueness is experienced in different ways, on the basis of different actions. To illustrate, in responding, I lift my hand; in telling a story, I speak for moments at a time. He distinguishes the capable self from the "exalted subject" (the Cartesian *cogito*) and the "humiliated subject" (the Nietzschean "anti-cogito").[7]

Defined as the "wounded cogito," it is a unique but fragile unity that persists only in so far as different activities (for example, speaking, acting, and narrating) are able to ground such a unity.[8]

Delineated as a more or less fragile unity, the capable self is cast as a phenomenon that must be interpreted and tested through available discourses. Granted his theoretical starting point in phenomenology where no particular discourse—science, literature, psychology, anthropology—is privileged a priori, Ricoeur settles on the language of literature and (as we will see in chapter 6) psychoanalysis as the most appropriate vehicle for self-understanding. What must be mediated through these discourses are four kinds of action that ground the identity of the self (as a unity of speech, a series of actions, a biographical narrative, and a moral agent). Narrative identity, which I will now examine, is the third form of the *ipse*-identity of the capable self.

NARRATIVE IDENTITY AND ARISTOTELIAN *MUTHOS*

In describing narrative identity as the third form of the *ipse*-identity of the capable self I digress somewhat from Ricoeur's stated views, at least from his stated views in some passages of the *OA*. In several of these, for example, he describes narrative identity as a form of mediation between *ipse* and *idem* identities.

> I hasten to complete my hypothesis: the polarity I am going to examine suggests an intervention of narrative identity in the conceptual constitution of personal identity in the manner of a specific mediator between the pole of character, where *idem* and *ipse* tend to coincide, and the pole of self-maintenance, where selfhood frees itself from sameness.[9]

However, viewing narrative identity as one kind of ipse-identity, and not as a mediator between *ipse* and *idem*-identities, is also, I suggest, consistent with his overall position. This is because, as I argued in chapter 4, Ricoeur radically distinguishes between the capable self with its *ipse*-identity and the real self with its *idem*-identity, describing them as "two modes of being" (and not two ends of a continuum). In my view, the relationship between *idem*- and *ipse*-identity should not be cast in terms of stability and change. *Idem*-identity, indeed, represents sameness which is, paradigmatically, associated with the perdurance of object-like entities such as the real self. But the stability of the latter can be opposed to the instability of a Humean (or Dennettian) or post-modern kind of selfhood. *Ipse*-identity, on the other hand, can be understood as a third alternative to either stability or fragmentation: it represents a form of temporal continuity, a fragile stability that is distinctively human. Granted that *ipse*-identity is not the opposite of *idem*-identity, narrative identity can be viewed as a form of *ipse*-identity which mediates, not between *idem* and *ipse*, but between *idem*-identity and instability. This is consistent with the following passage taken from the conclusion of *TN3*, "The difference between *idem* and *ipse* is nothing more than the difference between a substantial or formal identity and a narrative identity."[10] Here, Ricoeur explicitly states that *idem*-identity is a substantial identity relation while *ipse*-identity is a narrative identity relation. It is also consistent with his later pronouncements on narrative identity which distinguish between stability and instability on the one hand and narrative identity on the other, such as his claim: "I am stressing the expression 'narrative identity' for what we call subjectivity is neither an incoherent series of events nor an immutable substantiality, impervious to evolution. This is precisely the sort of identity which narrative composition alone can create through its dynamism."[11] The question arises, what kind of fragile stability does narrative identity offer?

Ricoeur's thesis is that the form of the story can successfully be applied to human lives, more specifically, that the narrative ordering of time and events provides unity and coherence to support the belief—sometimes strong, sometimes weak—that one persists as a unique self.

To state the identity of an individual or a community is to answer the question, "Who did this?" "Who is the agent, the author?" We first answer this question by naming someone, that is, by designating him or her with a proper name. But what is the basis for the permanence of this proper name? What justifies our taking the subject of an action, so designated by his, her, or its proper name, as the same throughout a life that stretches from birth to death? The answer has to be narrative. To answer the question "Who?" as Hannah Arendt has so forcefully put it, is to tell the story of a life. The story tells about the action of the "who."[12]

He translates the Aristotelian notion of *muthos* as emplotment to describe the narrative ordering that unifies the experiences and actions of an individual human being over time.[13] Such a unity is ultimately possible for Ricoeur because humans are temporal beings: Their lives are lived in time.

The concept of plot or *muthos* was initially deployed by Aristotle to explain the actions of characters in tragic plays. He privileges the form of the tragedy over other literary forms, such as poetry or comedy, because he argues that tragedy more closely imitates human action. In turn, he considers that the primary task of the tragic poet is to give primacy to plot over character or diction, because it is the plot that orders the action of the play. In the *Poetics*, Aristotle claims that:

Tragedy is essentially an imitation not of persons but of action and life. All human happiness or misery takes the form of action; the end for which we live is a certain kind of activity, not a quality. Character gives us qualities, but it is because of our actions that we are happy or the reverse. In a play accordingly they do not act in order to portray the characters; they include the characters for the sake of the action. So it is the action in it (or plot) that is the end and purpose of the tragedy; and the end is everywhere the chief thing. Besides this, a tragedy is impossible without action, but there might be one without Character.[14]

He prescribes the elements that are proper to the plot in the following way:

We have laid it down that a tragedy is an imitation of an action that is complete in itself, as a whole of some magnitude; for a whole may be of no magnitude to speak of. Now a whole is that which has beginning, middle and end. A beginning is that which is not itself necessarily after anything else, and which has naturally something else after it; an end is that which is naturally after something itself, either as its necessary or usual consequent, and with nothing else after it; and a middle, that which is by nature after one thing and has also another after it. A well-constructed plot, therefore, cannot either begin or end at any point one likes; beginning and end in it must be of the forms just described.[15]

So, tragedy imitates an action that is complete, whole, and of some magnitude. In addition, its "beginning," "middle," and "end" identify temporal divisions (as opposed to spatial divisions) that are necessarily connected with one another in the sense that they "cannot either begin or end at any point one likes." Amplifying this, Aristotle compares the unity of the plot with the "organic unity of a living creature."[16] He offers two ways of testing a sufficiently complete tragedy: memory and comprehension. It should be "of a length to be taken in by the memory," and that length must be consistent with its being comprehensible. He relates comprehension to the structure of the tragedy which should involve a number of stages through which the protagonist moves: "As a rough general formula, a length which allows of the hero passing by a series of probable or necessary stages from bad fortune to good, or from good to bad, may suffice as a limit for the magnitude of the story."[17] The probability or necessity involved in the hero's progress through the tragedy is made clear in another well-known passage where Aristotle presents the tragic plot as a depiction of the reversals of fortune and discoveries of the protagonist that produce a catharsis of pity or fear in the play's audience.[18] The achievement of cathartic release of either pity or fear is a mark of the success of any given play:

> It is evident from the above that the poet must be more the poet of his plots than of his verses, inasmuch as he is a poet by virtue of the imitative element in his work, and it is actions that he imitates. . . . Of simple plots and actions the episodic are the worst. I call a plot episodic when there is neither probability nor necessity in the sequence of its episodes. . . . Tragedy, however, is an imitation not only of a complete action, but also of incidents arousing pity and fear. Such incidents have the greatest effect on the mind when they

occur unexpectedly and at the same time in consequence of one another; there is more of the marvelous
in them than if they happened of themselves or by
mere chance. Even matters of chance seem most marvelous if there is an appearance of design as it were in
them; as for instance the statue of Mitys at Argos killed
the author of Mitys' death by falling down on him
when he was looking at it; for incidents like that we
think to be not without a meaning. A plot, therefore,
of this sort is necessarily finer than others.[19]

What is implicit in this account is that any successful
play must arouse human emotion as well as lend itself to
a rational explanation of the events that occur in it.
These events must be rendered as temporally structured,
necessarily connected, predictable, and designed.[20]
Moreover, for Aristotle, the good poet can make universal
claims about the nature of human kind in the sense that
he can imagine what might happen, and he can predict
what different kinds of men will say or do, given particular circumstances:

> The right thing, however, is in the characters just as in
> the incidents of the play to seek after the necessary or
> the probable; so that whenever such-and-such a per-
> sonage says or does such-and-such a thing, it shall be
> the necessary or the probable outcome of his char-
> acter; and whenever this incident follows on that, it
> shall be either the necessary or the probable conse-
> quence of it.[21]

Drawing inspiration from the Aristotelian project,

Ricoeur finds in the operation of emplotment a means of reconciling the seeming irreducible opposition between chronological time, or the "cosmic time" of a scientific stance, and the "human time" of a psychological or phenomenological stance.[22] Ricoeur's point is: Theories that measure chronological time (referring to linear time measured in instants by a clock) cannot adequately capture the relationship between human beings and time (for example, the "time of the soul" of Augustine's *Confessions* or the temporal depth of the Husserlian present weighted by past memories and future anticipations).[23] Ricoeur's thesis is that this opposition between cosmic and human time can be bridged because "time becomes human only when it is recounted," and "the passage by way of the narrative is the elevation of the time of the world to the time of man."[24] The Aristotelian account of the plot, according to Ricoeur, makes intelligible what would otherwise be a linear sequence of brute happenings, because the "configuring act" of emplotment unifies what is otherwise only episodic.[25] Through the operation of narrative emplotment, chronological time is humanized while human time captures features of objective time.[26]

Ricoeur's concept of emplotment, however, is far more dynamic and open-ended than its Aristotelian predecessor. While Aristotle, as outlined, was anxious that the tragedy close down meaning so that the actions of its characters were deemed inevitable and predictable, Ricoeur's understanding of emplotment as a narrative configuration or a "synthesis of the heterogeneous" opens up the way in which the plot operates at a number of different levels.[27] It connects diverse events within the temporal unity of the story, it reconciles disparate actions such as those that are intended, caused or random, in terms of their role in the progress of the story, and it displays a temporal form at the basis of events that is often non-chronological.[28] In relation to meaning, emplotment is not "a static structure" but "an operation, an integrating process, which . . . is completed only in the reader or in the spectator, that is to say, in the living receiver of the narrated story."[29] That its meaning is completed in the reader is a particularly important feature of Ricoeur's notion of emplotment. What it indicates is that the meaning of any story is never closed because it is partially dependent on the questions and focus that different readers bring to the story.

NARRATIVE RECOUNTING OF HUMAN LIVES

When Ricoeur transfers his understanding of *narrative emplotment* to the *narrative recounting* of actions and events of real life, he claims that it permits the interpretation, transformation, and intelligible understanding of what might otherwise be perceived as random, inconsistent, and contingent. In essence, the operation of narrative recounting involves treating the experiences and actions of an individual life—unintentional incidents, discoveries, triumphs and tragedies, chance or planned encounters, conflictual or collaborative interactions, successful or poor means to ends, and unintended results—

as a text that can be interpreted by the individual herself or by others.

Ricoeur claims that human action is similar to written texts because action comes from an agent as writing does from a writer and that, in so doing, it separates from her and acquires its own autonomy. Also, human actions leave behind a trace in time (for example, monuments, children, and bloodshed) just as texts leave traces such as documents or archives. Even more like a text, the significance of any given action is not limited to its initial occurrence but can be reinscribed in new frameworks of understanding at different times and by multiple interpreters:

> [H]uman action is in many ways a quasi-text. It is exteriorized in a manner comparable to the fixation characteristic of writing. In becoming detached from its agent, the action acquires an autonomy similar to the semantic autonomy of a text; it leaves a trace, a mark. It is inscribed in the course of things and becomes an archive and document. Even more like a text, of which the meaning has been freed from the initial conditions of its production, human action has a stature that is not limited to its importance for the situation in which it initially occurs, but allows it to be reinscribed in new social contexts. Finally, action, like a text, is an open work, addressed to an indefinite series of possible "readers." The judges are not contemporaries, but subsequent history.[30]

Delineating the self as a character in a play or novel, Ricoeur shifts emphasis away from the notion of the self as some kind of psychological interiority and expresses, instead, the dynamic and interpersonal nature of the self, its stability as well as its fragility, and its singularity as well as its dependence on a larger situation. Moreover, Ricoeur claims that "characters, we will say, are themselves plots," thus underlining the emplotted, dynamic, and relational nature of the self understood as a character in a story and distinguishing it from an account of character delineated in terms of dispositions and habits and viewed, largely, in terms of *idem* identity conditions (that is, some kind of persevering substance as discussed in Chapter 4).[31]

> Our life, when then embraced in a single glance, appears to us as the field of a constructive activity, borrowed from narrative understanding, by which we attempt to discover and not simply to impose from outside the *narrative identity which constitutes us*. I am stressing the expression "narrative identity" for what we call subjectivity is neither an incoherent series of events nor an immutable substantiality, impervious to evolution. This is precisely the sort of identity which narrative composition alone can create through its dynamism.[32]

For Ricoeur, the operation of narrative recounting provides a way of making the events of human lives intelligible that is different from the kind of intelligibility that scientists generally seek. The latter posit a causal model of explanation that explains any event in terms of antecedent events. Alternatively, narrative recounting posits a narrative order that connects disparate events in a new way that is distinct from logical or causal explanatory accounts. The nature of the unifying connection that narrative order establishes is the interpretation of human events as a part of a larger frame or story whereby each event becomes meaningful in relation to the whole and vice versa.[33] Thus the intelligibility of the "narrative event" is explained in terms of the whole, while the intelligibility of "objective events" (as articulated by scientific explanation) are explained in terms of prior causes:

> The essential difference distinguishing the narrative model from every other model of connectedness resides in the status of events, which we have repeatedly made the touchstone of the analysis of the self. Whereas in a causal-type model, event and occurrence are indiscernible, the narrative event is defined by its relation to the very operation of configuration; it participates in the unstable structure of discordant discordance characteristic of the plot itself. [34]

What is paradoxical about the way in which emplotment, alternatively described as configuration, operates in a story is that it can change the status of the events that take place in the story from contingent to necessary. On the causal model, a surprising event that takes place at the culmination of a prior course of events could be explained as contingent, to indicate that the prior series of events could have turned out differently. On the narrative model, however, the same event may be construed as a necessary and inevitable outcome if its consequences are taken into consideration and it is considered from the vantage of time. In a nutshell, narrative explanation not only considers what happens before, but also what happens *after* an event, as relevant to understanding that event.

> The paradox of emplotment is that it inverts the effect of contingency, in the sense of that which could have happened differently, or which might not have happened at all, by incorporating it in some way into the effect of necessity or probability exerted by the configuring act. The inversion of the effect of contingency into an effect of necessity is produced at the very core of the event: as a mere occurrence, the latter is confined to thwarting the expectations created by the prior course of events; it is quite simply the unexpected, the surprising. It only becomes an integral part of the story when understood after the fact, once it is transfigured by the so-to-speak retrograde necessity which proceeds from the temporal totality carried to its term.[35]

What distinguishes Ricoeur's narrative model of explanation from the traditional causal one (and, incidentally, the Aristotelian one) is that it seeks to enlarge rather than reduce the number of possible causes that can be posited as engendering any specific event. In this way, the narrative model captures the everyday experience of individuals who are wont to interpret and re-interpret the events in their lives from different temporal perspectives. For example, an individual, at 40 years, may view a particular experience—a win in the lottery—as a lucky break in a series of thwarted efforts to earn money. The same individual, at 60, may view the same lottery win as the origin of a series of transformations leading up to their current unhappiness. Thus, a sequence of human events may be causally explained—the whys and hows of the lottery win—but the significance of the sequence of events taken as a whole is not fully explained in this way.[36] On the narrative view, actions are made intelligible by uniting action and consequences. Specifically, the consequences, whether intended or not, foreseen or not, produce additional meaning to someone.

It follows that the narrative self is fragile for a number of reasons, not least, because such a unity is not readily determined by the chronological ordering of one's own life:

> Now there is nothing in real life that serves as a narrative beginning; memory is lost in the hazes of early childhood; my birth and, with greater reason, the act through which I was conceived belong more to the history of others—in this case, to my parents—than to me. As for my death, it will finally be recounted only in the stories of those who survive me.[37]

Granted the gap between narrative and "real" life, which I will discuss in more detail in chapter 6, Ricoeur nevertheless argues that it can be partly bridged because of the way in which we understand ourselves through the narratives that are made available to us by our culture: "An unbridgeable difference does remain, but this difference is partially abolished by our power of applying to ourselves the plots that we have received from our culture and of trying on the different roles assumed by the favorite characters of the stories most dear to us."[38] Consider the way in which stories of death might prepare us for our own death, or the way in which our fictional heroes—Lara Croft, James Bond, or Elizabeth Bennett—model various gender or human possibilities.

Such an account of narrative identity can be distinguished from that of Alasdair MacIntyre who also construes the self narratively but not in terms of the narrative intelligibility found in stories or plays about fictional lives. On MacIntyre's account, the meaning of an individual's life story is made intelligible through understanding the various roles she plays in her community:

> In what does the unity of an individual life consist? The answer is that its unity is the unity of a narrative embodied in a single life. To ask "What is the good for me?" is to ask how best I might live out that unity and bring it to completion. To ask "What is the good for man?" is to ask what all answers to the former question must have in common. But now it is important to emphasize that it is the systematic asking of these two questions and the attempt to answer them in deed as well as in word which provide the moral life with its unity. The unity of a human life is the unity of a narrative quest. [39]

Unlike MacIntyre, who ultimately appeals to commonly held traditions and values in search of narrative intelligibility, Ricoeur argues that it is possible to compose several diverse plots about a human life, and that the meaning of any given set of events can vary for the individual concerned as well as for any other narrator or reader of them: "Just as it is possible to compose several plots on the subject of the same incidents (which, thus, should not really be called the same events), so it is always possible to weave different, even opposed, plots about our lives."[40] On this view, narrative identity is a provisional and revisable unity that is woven from the many plots and activities of a single life.

> In the same way, we never cease to reinterpret the narrative identity that constitutes us, in the light of the narratives proposed to us by our culture.... It is in this way that we learn to become the *narrator* and the hero *of our own story*, without actually becoming the *author of our own life.* We can apply to ourselves the concept of *narrative voices* which constitute the symphony of great works such as epics, tragedies, dramas and novels. The difference is that in all these works it is the author who is disguised as the narrator and who wears the mask of the various characters and, among all of these, the mask of the dominant voice that tells the story we read. We can become our own narrator, in imitation of these narrative voices, without being able to become the author.... It is therefore by means of the imaginative variations of our own ego that we attempt to obtain a narrative understanding of ourselves, the only kind that escapes the apparent choice between sheer change and absolute identity.[41]

This understanding takes a middle ground between "absolute identity" on the one hand, and "sheer change" on the other. On Ricoeur's account, an individual can imitate various culturally available narrative voices, and he can be the narrator and the hero of his stories, but he is not the author of his life, the "dominant voice" controlling his passage.

IPSE-IDENTITY AND LITERARY PUZZLE CASES

Cast as one form of the *ipse*-identity of the capable self, narrative identity, according to Ricoeur, provides a better solution to the problem of personal identity than either traditional Lockean or contemporary naturalist alternatives. Ricoeur directly refers to the Cartesian-inspired Lockean solution to personal identity: "[T]he narrative operation has developed an entirely original concept of dynamic identity which reconciles the same categories that Locke took as contraries: identity and diversity."[42] Ricoeur objects to Locke's account of personal identity on two separate grounds: (1) that it explicitly advances the *idem*-identity conditions of the real self, but implicitly appeals to the *ipse*-identity conditions of the capable self, and (2) that the identity conditions of spatio-temporal objects and the identity conditions of the self are of a different order.[43]

Specifically, in the fifth study of *OA* and also in his essay, "Narrative Identity," Ricoeur challenges Derek Parfit's neo-Lockean solution to the problem of personal identity.[44] Parfit's thesis is that personal identity over time can be fully explained by reference to a set of facts (psychological and/or physical continuity), and he rejects what he calls the "Further Fact View" which posits personal identity as a "Cartesian Pure Ego, or pure spiritual substance"—a further fact that cannot be explained by physical and/or psychological continuity. Ricoeur's main objection to the Parfitian thesis is that it ignores the possibility that the self can be conceived in terms other than as a "thing" or "further fact." He argues that the gap between Parfit's reductionist account and our ordinary belief that the self is a separate, determinate, persisting, and morally significant entity opens up because Parfit limits the understanding of identity to *idem,* or sameness, and fails to acknowledge the second kind of personal identity which Ricoeur argues is important—*ipse,* or selfhood. He supports his claim by analyzing the different ways in which the thought experiments of science and the limit cases of literary fiction treat the self. In brief, he claims that literary fiction offers a range of different models of the self that, however diverse and insubstantial, can, nevertheless, be seen to persist in time because of their *ipse*-identity. Alternatively, he argues that the thought experiments of science, which focus solely on the *idem*-identity conditions of the self, yield only indeterminate and counter-intuitive accounts of the self.

I will examine this perspective in a little more detail. One commonly held belief regarding personal identity is that a person's identity can be unambiguously determined as persisting or not. For example, we might believe, either, that the person who had cornflakes for breakfast this morning is the same person as the one who is typing on the computer this afternoon, *or*, that she is not. Questions of identity appear to be decidable in terms of a "yes" or "no." Parfit rejects this belief and argues for the indeterminacy of identity on the basis of the possibility of the brain being divided, transplanted, or replicated in some way. In the Parfitian account of brain replication that Ricoeur discusses, two thought experiments are envisaged. In both, an exact copy of Parfit's brain is sent via radio to Mars where a replica of him is constituted. In the first case, what Parfit calls the case of *simple transportation*, his brain and body on earth are destroyed during the process. The question arises as to whether he survives in his replica. On the one hand, they are numerically distinct; on the other hand, they are qualitatively identical. It would seem that the case cannot be decided.[45] In the second case, what Parfit calls *the branch-line case*, his brain and body on earth are not immediately destroyed, but his heart is damaged. When he subsequently talks to his replica on Mars, the replica promises to love his wife, care for his children, and finish his book. The question that arises here is whether or not Parfit should find this consoling. On the one hand, if the replica is considered to be distinct from him, then his prospect on the branch-line is almost as bad as death. If, however, the replica is "the same as him" in some significant way, then having a replica is "about as good as ordinary survival."[46] In a sense, Parfit is saying that he will not live, but neither does he die.

Parfit's deployment of puzzle cases is a strategic move, according to Ricoeur, because the puzzle cases that have emerged with the aid of science fiction *tend to* give rise to indeterminate responses. He describes Parfit's dilemma as a paradox of sameness where the question, "Am I going to survive?" is posited as equivalent to the question, "Will there be a person who will be the *same* person as I?" Parfit resolves the question only by considering it vacuous. In each of the cases discussed, none of the surviving individuals can properly be said to be the *same* as me.[47] Thus Parfit concludes that questions regarding our notion of personal identity are empty and this implies that it is not identity in the usual sense that matters.[48]

Ricoeur argues, however, that the Parfitian conclusion that questions of personal identity are empty can be resisted. It is inevitable, only if one holds that what counts as identity is *idem*-identity or sameness. Ricoeur has an alternative strategy, one which counts identity as *ipse*-identity or selfhood and relies on puzzle cases drawn from literature rather than science fiction. (Note that Ricoeur takes it for granted that a viable distinction between the puzzle cases of science fiction and the puzzle cases of literary fiction can be made. Nowhere, for example, does he acknowledge that science fiction is itself a particular literary genre. For present purposes of clarity, I accept Ricoeur's rather crude distinction because what is at stake regarding them is the content of the puzzle cases themselves, not the finer points of their place in the literary canon. I take a more critical view of this distinction in chapter 7.)

Ricoeur argues that the puzzle cases of literary fiction give rise to a different kind of indeterminacy to those of scientific thought experiments. He points out that literary fiction offers a number of different models of the self that correspond with different literary genres. For example, in folklore and fairy tales the character is largely unchanging and, as such, readily identifiable and reidentifiable as the same. Alternatively, the classic novel, by authors such as Tolstoy or Austen, posits a character whose sameness does not entirely disappear even though they go through major transformations in the course of the novel. Or, in the stream of consciousness novels of Virginia Woolf or James Joyce, for example, the character is presented in a very fragmented and indefinite way.[49] Ricoeur also refers to Robert Musil's *L'homme sans qualités* ("The Man without Qualities") whose protagonist endures such a crisis of identity as to become unidentifiable in the usual sense. It is interesting that in this, as in many other insights, Aristotle was there before Ricoeur. The former also acknowledged that the "modern" tragedies of his time also sacrificed the development of character to the elaboration of plot:

> Besides this, a tragedy is impossible without action, but there might be one without Character. The tragedies of most of *the moderns* are characterless—a characteristic common among poets of all kinds, and with its counterpart in painting in Zeuxis as compared with Polygnotus; for whereas the latter is strong in character, the work of Zeuxis is devoid of it. . . . We maintain, therefore, that the first essential, the life and soul, so to speak, of tragedy is the plot; and the characters come second—compare the parallel in painting, where the most beautiful colors laid on without order will not give one the same pleasure as a simple black-and-white sketch of a portrait.[50]

What the limit cases of the modern novel reveal for Ricoeur is a sense of identity that is not exhausted by sameness (that is, by a list of characteristics or properties that are identified and re-identified). In the case of *L'homme sans qualités*, the response to the question, "Who am I" is not empty or meaningless if the answer is "nothing." For there remains the one who asks the question, to whom "nothing" is a meaningful, if even disconcerting, response:

> With regard to the category of the subject, a non-subject is not nothing. Indeed, we would not be interested in this drama of dissolution and we would not be thrown into confusion by it if the non-subject were not still a figure of the subject, even in the negative mode. Let us suppose someone poses the question, "who am I?" Even if nothing or almost nothing is the response, this is still a response to the question who, simply reduced to the nakedness of the question itself.[51]

In peeling apart the two senses of identity—*idem* and *ipse*—literary fiction renders a different response to the question of personal identity, one that posits the asking of the question, "Who am I" as a feature of the identity of the capable self that cannot be erased by filling out the answers to it. Ricoeur argues that *L'homme sans qualités* is better translated as the *The Man without Properties* in order to underline that such a self lacks sameness but not selfhood: "What is now lost, under the title of 'property,' is what allowed us to equate the character in the story with lasting dispositions or character."[52] What is significant, for Ricoeur, about such a character is that he is cast in such a way that his continued existence as a self is meaningful even though that continuing self does not seem to share any of the qualities or characteristics of an earlier self.

Ricoeur's strategy is to start from the place of questioning: For him, it is the reflexive nature of human beings that prompts them to ask questions about identity, and this is foundational. The insight is a powerful one to which I will return in chapter 7 because it directly challenges the accepted view of many critical and psychological theorists that autobiography and biography provide evidence of the fragmented character of human selves.[53] Even in the case of Musil's "characterless" character, Ricoeur makes the case that the novel's protagonist holds on to a sense of self in as much as he can raise a question about his own existence. In sum, his central claim is that human beings are such that they raise questions about their own individual existence, and importantly, that those questions arise prior to any definite ontological commitments about, or descriptions of, whatever features may be considered to apply to them. Therefore, he concludes that while technological limit cases may undermine the determinacy of the self, understood as substantial, literary fiction captures the reflexive condition of the human being and reframes the problem of determinacy in relation to the self, understood as capable.

The second advantage Ricoeur sees in the deployment of puzzle cases drawn from literature is that the characters in plays and novels share a second element of the human condition: corporeality. He posits human embodiment as an "insurpassable mediation between the self and the world."[54] In contrast, he claims that the thought experiments of a naturalist approach are constructed out of a "technological dream" wherein the brain can be substituted for the person and the "corporeity, as we know it, in joy and in suffering" is taken as a contingent variable.[55] For Ricoeur, while replication may be neither logically nor physically impossible in principle, it violates another order which precedes existing rules, laws and facts. He is arguing for an understanding of the person as a being whose condition it is to be *rooted on this earth* in such a way as to make it impossible to uproot, manipulate, or transplant her in the way in which Parfit's, and indeed Dennett's, thought experiments envisage: "The question will be whether they do not violate a constraint of another order, *concerning human rootedness on this earth*. . . . these are highly technological manipulations performed on the brain, taken as equivalent to the person."[56] It is unclear what Ricoeur means by the term "rootedness," but I take it to imply that the embodied and located existence of each human being is unrepeatable and irreplaceable. Specifically, he would reject Dennett's equivalence of the brain with the person because, for Ricoeur, the way in which human beings are embodied has particular implications for the way in which the world opens up to each human individual. Think of a very simple example: height, a feature of human existence that is taken for granted in daily life.

While the species as a whole bears a relation with

the earth in terms of gravity and perspective, each human being has a unique relationship, one which would be radically altered for her if she were suddenly confined to a wheel chair or to bed. The same considerations apply if one considers changes in weight, or the height and weight margins between the sexes, or, indeed, the sexes themselves.

Take a second example, drawn from science fiction, specifically, from a film called *The Matrix* released in 1999. One of the many philosophically interesting feats of the main protagonist, Neo, played by Keanu Reeves, is that he is able to interface with a computer program and "download" information of varying complexity into his brain. One of the programs he downloads, and thereby immediately becomes expert on, is a particularly advanced form of martial art. The practice of interfacing between brains and computers and downloading of expertise, if technologically possible, is theoretically acceptable *vis-à-vis* Dennett's puzzle cases on personal identity outlined above. It fits neatly, for example, with Dennett's discussion on immortality where, according to him, one's immortality might be guaranteed by the downloading of one's narratives into a computer. However, it is not consistent with Ricoeur's position because, according to it, the process of acquiring information (of any kind, but, all the more so, of this kind) invokes a holistic corporeal engagement. From a Ricoeurian perspective, the idea of downloading information, as happens in Neo's case, presupposes a component view of mind. Ricoeur's account of corporeality excludes the possibility that one cognitive component can be added to the brain without entailing enormous disruption. On his account, corporeality is a cohesive unity that opens up a world. For example, the process of acquiring the expertise of a martial art means that the life; posture; outlook; and intellectual, emotional, and physical style of the individual under instruction would radically change. In fantasy, this may be achieved at the press of a button, but such a fantasy takes the viewer very far away from the actual conditions of human life.

In short, the specific ways in which human beings are embodied predispose them to engage with the world in particular ways. Human beings do not learn to sing, swim, ride bicycles, use chopsticks, and multiply numbers and children, instantaneously nor cerebrally. Instead, learning, growing, acting and interacting in the world involves being located in time and space and taking up time and space. The fact that a human being is temporally and spatially engaged not only constrains her but also enables her to view herself as a persisting self. While it may be granted that accounts (such as those of Dennett's or Parfit's) of the manipulation and substitution of brains undermine the stability of the self, understood as substantial, literary fictional accounts of the human condition, as an embodied and active engagement with the world, lend support to the stability of the self, understood as capable.

CERTAINTY, KNOWLEDGE AND ATTESTATION

In sum, Ricoeur argues that the identity of the capable self is secured on the basis of appeal to four different capacities: speaking, acting, narrating, and assuming moral responsibility. Of the four, he focuses on narrative capacity and argues that the self is unified through the narrative ordering of the life events of an individual and that this is made possible because of the temporal nature of human existence. He further argues that if the capable self is understood through the lens of literature rather than science, the limit cases of the former ground the identity of the self in features of human existence such as reflexivity and corporeality.

However, as Ricoeur himself acknowledges, the self may be more or less unified—more or less stable or fragile—on the basis of the four capacities. The problem arises as to how much or how little of these capacities has to be present in order to support the claim that a given individual is a single persisting self. Ricoeur's solution is to appeal to what he calls "attestation" which, he argues, "constitutes the instance of judgment that stands over against suspicion, in all of those circumstances where the self designates itself, either as the author of what is said, or as the agent of an action, or as the narrator of a tale, or as the subject accountable for its acts."[57] Ricoeur's claim is that the assurance that a self persists can be tested with regard to each of the four activities of the capable self: (1) the power of speaking (verbal), (2) the power of doing, (3) the power to tell a biographical story, and (4) the power to assume responsibility.[58]

So, what exactly is this "attestation"? To begin with, Ricoeur does not explicitly and comprehensively amplify and defend it. The notion is initially delineated in the introduction to *OA*, implied throughout the studies and developed further in the tenth study. It is also implied in his defense of psychoanalytic claims in *Freud and Philosophy* and *Hermeneutics and the Human Sciences*.[59] Nevertheless, because, in my view, it is critical to his overall theory of the self, I will attempt to unravel its key features and their implications for his account of the self.

I understand attestation, in general, to be the level of certainty that can be attributed to claims that link the phenomenological emphasis on direct experience with the hermeneutic understanding of the world as interpreted. It relates to Ricoeur's overall metaphysical position, already analyzed in chapter 4, and summarized in the following passage:

> The final accent placed on the category of hope certainly marks my distance in relation to security and to the guarantees that an ontology of being-in-itself would provide for thinking. I am far removed indeed from this type of metaphysics. But my major concern has never been to know if and how I could survive the deconstruction of metaphysics "itself"; it has been instead to do metaphysics in another manner, on the basis, precisely, of a hermeneutics phenomenology.[60]

In this passage, Ricoeur distances his thesis from the secure or guaranteed foundations of traditional metaphysics. However, accepting that a task of philosophy is to seek a coherence of some kind, he opts instead to redirect metaphysical enquiry and privileges what he calls the "category of hope."[61]

Ricoeur's deployment of the psychological category of "hope" to characterize his position and his designation of attestation as the level of certainty he can expect with regard to his claims about the world need to be unraveled. First, he considers three existing approaches to truth: a Cartesian kind of certainty, nihilism, and radical doubt or suspicion. The first seeks foundational truths. The second, equally, makes ultimate claims, but these assert the meaninglessness of existence. The third raises doubts about the status of every kind of claim. In relation to these three, Ricoeur places hermeneutic attestation as a level of certainty that is directly opposed to the third category of radical doubt or suspicion.[62] In sum, faced with adopting any of the metaphysical views (1) that ultimate truths exist, (2) that there is no truth and that life is meaningless, or (3) that we must doubt everything, attestation offers a fourth alternative for Ricoeur; that our lives bear meaning for us. This fourth alternative amounts to a choice between suspicion (that everything must be doubted) and faith (that the world and our experiences are meaningful to each one of us).

I apply the term "faith" with care here and appeal to Ricoeur's secular understanding of it when he applied it to history: "Faith in meaning, but in a meaning hidden from history, is thus both the courage to believe in a profound significance of the most tragic history (and therefore a feeling of confidence and resignation in the very heart of conflict) and a certain rejection of system and fanaticism, a sense of the *open*."[63] So, faith involves courage, confidence, and a coming to terms with human tragedy. It further combines a rejection of foundational systems and the possibility of absolute certainty with an openness to the possibility that one's own life is, nevertheless, meaningful. The question arises, however, as to what Ricoeur means by attributing "profound significance" to human lives; encouraging "confidence," "hope," and "resignation"; and advocating openness, in opposition to foundationalism or nihilism. If Ricoeur is not to be accused here of falling back on some kind of theism to underlie such "faith," then an alternative warrant for his optimism must be found.

My own view is that Ricoeur's position is not so much naively optimistic or theistic as it is theoretically prior to the oppositional positions of foundationalism, relativism, or nihilism. In essence, Ricoeur's thesis is that any position we assume with regard to the world and ourselves, be it scientific naturalism, theism, or nihilism, is mediated. As such, no absolute or objective view is possible, and equally, the nihilism that follows in the wake of such absolutist views is also impossible. What is fundamental, if anything is fundamental, is the operation of interpretation. If I define interpretation as an operation that seeks meanings, unities, and coherencies in the world, then it is legitimate to describe the life of the interpreter as one that involves "hope" and "faith" without committing oneself to theism. This construal of his position as one of non-theistic optimism is supported by Ricoeur's account of self-attestation, which I will now outline.

SELF-UNDERSTANDING AND SELF-ATTESTATION

Applied to understanding the self, Ricoeur opposes the notion of attestation, defined as an "alethic (or veritative) mode," to Cartesian "hypercertainty," Nietzschean skepticism, and naturalist empiricism.[64] First of all, he argues that an explanation of the activities of doubting or thinking is not achieved by the positing of the *cogito*.[65] His argument is that the Cartesian ambition to establish it as a "final, ultimate, foundation" is responsible for the elevation of the *cogito* as a "first truth" on the one hand and a "vast illusion" on the other. The strength of the ambition is revealed in the radical nature of the doubt to which the subject is pressed. This doubt is subsequently applied to all epistemological paradigms including common sense, the mathematical and physical sciences, and the tradition of philosophy. Each is reduced to the status of opinion by a single strategy: the hypothesis of an evil genius who may deceive with regard to the seemingly simplest of calculations such as the addition of two and three.[66] The Cartesian project is to affirm certainty in the face of doubt, and the more radical the doubt raised and refuted, the greater the certainty thereby affirmed.

Claiming that the radical skepticism of the Cartesian variety must inevitably lead to a radical self-annihilation, Ricoeur specifically examines the conclusions that Nietzsche draws from it. Nietzsche's general thesis is that language is inescapably figurative, in other words, facts about the world do not exist prior to or outside of a language that seeks to represent them more or less successfully. The conclusion that he draws from this is that the difference between true claims and false claims about the world cannot be established. In a footnote, Ricoeur cites the following passage from Nietzsche that illuminates this view,

> What then is truth? A movable host of metaphors, metonymies, and anthropomorphisms: in short, a sum of human relations which have been poetically and rhetorically intensified, transferred, and embellished, and which, after long usage, seem to a people to be fixed, canonical, and binding. Truths are illusions which we have forgotten as illusions; they are metaphors that have become worn out and have been drained of sensuous force, coins which have lost their embossing and are now considered as metal and no longer as coins.[67]

Nietzsche's thesis, applied to knowledge claims that are derived from the *cogito* reflecting on its own operations, entails that the *cogito* becomes its own evil genius. While for Descartes the *cogito* may doubt that it is waking or dreaming and still *know* that it doubts, for Nietzsche the *cogito* has no such assurance. Doubting is *itself* suspect. For Neitzsche, we must be just as suspicious of the phenomena of the internal world as we are of the phenomena of the external world. On this account, he observes:

> I am convinced of . . . the phenomenalism of the inner world also: everything that reaches our consciousness is utterly and completely adjusted, simplified, schema-

tized, interpreted, the actual process of inner "perception," the relation of causes between thoughts, feelings, desires, between subject and object, is absolutely
concealed from us, and may be purely imaginary.[68]

In addition to opposing attestation to Cartesian certainty
and Nietzschean suspicion, Ricoeur also distinguishes
what he sees as the weaker requirements of attestation
from the criteria of validation applied in the natural sciences:

> To my mind, attestation defines the sort of certainty that
> hermeneutics may claim, not only with respect to the
> epistemic exaltation of the cogito in Descartes, but also
> with respect to its humiliation in Nietzsche and his suc-
> cessors. ... What is set in opposition to attestation is fun-
> damentally the notion of *episteme*, of science, taken in
> the sense of ultimate and self-founding knowledge.[69]

Epistemologically, for example, he argues that there is no
parallel between the statements: "I grasp with my hands"
and "I think with my brain"—they appeal to two kinds of
knowledges, one learned from direct experience, one
objectively demonstrated.[70] Specifically, he wonders if
neuroscientific knowledge has anything to add to
existing knowledge of direct experience:

> Something happens in my brain, and when you tell
> me what happens in my brain, you add to my knowl-
> edge of the base, of the underlying reality; but does
> this knowledge help me in trying to decipher the
> enigma of a face? Do you believe that you understand

the faces of others in the street, in your family, because you know something about what happens in their brains?[71]

So, what exactly does attestation involve? Ricoeur describes it as a kind of credence, testimony, or belief that stands mid-way between opinion and truth:

> Attestation, presents itself first, in fact, as a kind of belief. But it is not a doxic belief, in the sense in which *doxa* (belief) has less standing than *episteme* (science, or better, knowledge). Whereas doxic belief is implied in the grammar of "I believe-that," attestation belongs to the grammar of "I believe in." It thus links up with testimony, as the etymology reminds us, inasmuch as it is in the speech of the one giving testimony that one believes. One can call upon no epistemic instance any greater than that of the belief—or, if one prefers, the credence.[72]

And, acknowledging his debt to Hegel and Heidegger, he posits attestation as an equivalent of the notion of conscience:[73]

> [C]onscience appears as the inner assurance that, in some particular circumstance, sweeps away doubt, hesitation, the suspicion of inauthenticity, hypocrisy, self-complacence, and self-deception, and authorizes the acting and suffering human being to say: here I stand.[74]

In this passage, attestation is described as a stance one can take in opposition to, and in spite of, factors such as doubt, inauthenticity, smugness, and self-deception. The assurance of attestation, he claims, "remains the *ultimate recourse* against all suspicion."[75] Even though, for Ricoeur, "[c]onscience-attestation seems to inscribe itself in the problematic of truth, both as credence and commitment," he nevertheless acknowledges a limit to the level of truth that may be determined.[76] Two separate comments he makes in this regard are worth noting:

1. Precisely, attestation escapes sight, if sight is expressed in propositions held to be true or false. Veracity is not truth, in the sense of the adequation of knowledge to its object.[77]
2. This point is that a human being has no mastery over the inner, intimate certitude of existing as a self; this is something that comes upon us, like a gift, a grace that is not at our disposal. This non-mastery of a voice that is more heard than spoken leaves intact the question of its origin.[78]

The first passage argues that attestation is not an operation of perception as deciphered in epistemological claims about the world that have a truth value. In the second, Ricoeur concedes that any intimate certainty we have at any time that we exist as a self is fragile. This second passage may be read by some as echoing a Christian belief in human life as a gift from God that is granted or denied according to his will and not ours. This reading is certainly plausible, and as such it provides insight into what fuels Ricoeur's determination to locate some basis for a unified self. However, I view it as a restatement of his hermeneutic belief that meaning and authorship are not the same, and that we describe our selves *after* the detour of interpretation, not before. The detour opens up a gap between the human being who seeks self-understanding and the way in which the self is eventually conceived. The self that is the outcome of the interpretative detour is tested or attested on the basis of reliability and thus is constantly threatened by its contrary suspicion, "and there is no recourse against suspicion but a more reliable attestation."[79]

Applied to self-knowledge or self-understanding, then, Ricoeur's process of attestation eschews the standards of validation that analytic philosophical positions lay claim to—rationalist principles and scientific research. Instead, attestation focuses on direct experience and validates it in terms such as testimony, veracity, and reliability, as well as their opposites: hypocrisy, self-deception, and inconsistency.

To recap: In this chapter, I have argued that the success of Ricoeur's account of the capable self depends, in part, on whether or not he can successfully determine the conditions of its continuity over time. As we have seen, Ricoeur's strategy with regard to the problem of personal identity is to first of all question what is involved in establishing the identity of a phenomenon such as the self (as opposed to the identity of spatio-temporal objects). Second, he argues that the persistence of the self as he understands it—as capable—is determined on the basis of the capacity of any given human being to speak, act, narrate, and assume moral responsibility. Taking the third of these capacities, Ricoeur argues that if we take an individual human life as a text and interpret it in terms of certain narrative standards of plausibility and intersubjective credibility, then any given account of the self that meets with these standards may be viewed as an account of a single continuous unity. In addition, he draws on puzzle cases from literary fiction to give force to his argument and to distinguish his account of the self and his view of its identity from naturalist alternatives. Finally, Ricoeur introduces attestation as an interpretative approach that contributes to but cannot exhaust self-understanding.

On this reading of his project, Ricoeur provides us with an alternative approach to the problem of the self and its continuity over time that is innovative, comprehensive, and philosophically basic. In short, Ricoeur offers a new perspective on a very old problem—the problem of personal identity. His account is also thorough in that he addresses each of the traditional concerns regarding the self and its identity: the conditions of identity as well as the order of truth against which they should be tested. Finally, it is philosophically basic in the sense that Ricoeur's account of attestation describes a way of understanding the world of direct experience, which is prior to rationalist or objectivist standards of truth. What remains to be done is to narrow the focus in the next chapter to his specific account of *narrative attestation*.

NOTES TO CHAPTER 5

1. In the Conclusion of *TN*3, Ricoeur acknowledges that narrative identity does not exhaust the question of the "self-constancy of a subject" (p. 249). And in *OA*, for example, while studies 5 and 6 construe the self narratively, Ricoeur examines the linguistic possibilities of selfhood in studies 1 and 2; the self in action in studies 3 and 4; and the self as moral agent in studies 7, 8, and 9.

2. Ricoeur in Changeux and Ricoeur, *What Makes Us Think?* p. 29. Ontological dualism describes the Cartesian view that a human being comprises two distinct substances: body and soul.

3. Ibid., pp. 15–16.

4. Ricoeur, "From Psychoanalysis to the Question of the Self, or Thirty Years of Philosophical Work," p. 89. Ricoeur does not explicitly use the term "capable self" in *OA*. However, it is implicitly invoked by the structure of the *OA*, which addresses the speaking, acting, narrating, and imputing subject, and also by an early passage in the *OA* which describes his enterprise as a practical philosophy whose focus is human action—specifically the actions of describing, narrating, and prescribing (p. 19).

5. Ricoeur in Changeux and Ricoeur, *What Makes Us Think?* p. 214. He also discusses the idea of the "capable subject" as the basis for moral autonomy in *The Just*, pp. 1–10.

6. Ricoeur, *The Just*, p. 84.

7. Ricoeur, *OA*, pp. 23ff; "Intellectual Autobiography," pp. 23–24.

8. Ibid.

9. Ricoeur, *OA*, pp. 118–19. See also *OA*, pp. 124, 165–66 and "From Psychoanalysis to the Question of the Self, or Thirty Years of Philosophical Work," p. 89 for similar descriptions. See

Bernard P. Dauenhauer, "Ricoeur and Political Identity," in *Paul Ricoeur and Narrative*, ed. Morny Joy (Alberta: University of Calgary Press, 1997), pp. 130-131 for a development of this view of narrative identity.

10. Ricoeur, *TN*3, p. 246.

11. Paul Ricoeur, "Life in Quest of Narrative," in *On Paul Ricoeur, Narrative and Interpretation*, ed. David Wood (London: Routledge, 1991), p. 32.

12. Ricoeur, *TN*3, p. 246.

13. Ricoeur acknowledges that Aristotle's term *muthos* signifies both fable (an imaginary story) and plot (a well-constructed story) and takes the latter meaning for the purposes of his project.

14. Aristotle, "Poetics," in *The Complete Works of Aristotle* 2, ed. Jonathan Barnes, Bollingen Series LXXI (Princeton, NJ: Princeton University Press, 1984), 6 1450a 16-25.

15. Ibid., 7 1450b 25-1451a 10.

16. Ibid., 23 1459a1 20.

17. Ibid., 7 1451a1 15.

18. Aristotle cites an example from Sophocles' tragedy *Oedipus Rex*. In the play, a reversal of fortune comes about when the messenger, intending to remove Oedipus's fears regarding his mother, inadvertently reveals the secret of his birth. Following on this, Oedipus discovers the true situation and the audience in turn feels pity for his plight. Aristotle defines the process of discovery in the following way: "A discovery is, as the very word implies, a change from ignorance to knowledge, and thus to either love or hate, in the personages marked for good or evil fortune" (*Poetics*, 11 1452a1 30).

19. Ibid., 9 1451b 25-1452a 10.

20. Aristotle regularly refers to *Oedipus Rex* as an example of his analysis of the tragic form. J. Hillis Miller interestingly describes Oedipus as the reasoner *extraordinaire*:

He incarnates the desire to see to the bottom of things. He also is a surrogate for the rationality of the reader or spectator who wants to understand the action of the play, to see and comprehend what is revealed by that action. Oedipus is patiently and doggedly reasonable in trying to think things out on the basis of the evidence he is given. He is the incarnation of the desire to know, at all costs (J. Hillis Miller, *Reading Narrative* [Oklahoma: Oklahoma University Press, 1998], pp. 13-14).

21. Aristotle, *Poetics,* 15 1454a1 35.

22. Ricoeur, *OA,* p. 143 fn.4.

23. Ricoeur, *TN3,* pp. 61, 104-126.

24. Ricoeur, "From Psychoanalysis to the Question of the Self, or Thirty Years of Philosophical Work," p. 80.

25. Ricoeur explains *concordance* as "the principle of order that presides over what Aristotle calls 'the arrangement of facts,'" *discordances* as "the reversals of fortune that make the plot an ordered transformation from an initial situation to a terminal situation," and *configuration* as the "art of composition which mediates between concordance and discordance" (Ricoeur, *OA,* p. 141).

26. A paradigm example of this is *Oedipus Rex* where the physical action of the play (Oedipus's abandonment as a baby, his murder of his father, his solving of the Sphinx's riddle, and his sleeping with his mother) has already taken place before the play begins, and the play itself involves a series of conversations which lead Oedipus to discover what he has done.

27. Ricoeur, *Time and Narrative* 1 (*TN*1), trans. Kathleen Blamey and David Pellauer (Chicago: University of Chicago Press, 1984), p. ix. Originally published as *Temps et Récit* 1 (Paris: Editions du Seuil, 1982).

28. Just as the beginning of a tragedy for Aristotle is determined by the poet, and his choice of beginning determines the
signification of the entire play, so the plot of any novel for
Ricoeur does not necessarily begin on the first page or end on
the last page of the book in which it is written.

28. Ricoeur, "Life in Quest of Narrative," p. 21.

29. Paul Ricoeur, "Explanation and Understanding: On
Some Remarkable Connections Among the Theory of the Text,
Theory of Action, and Theory of History," in *The Philosophy of
Paul Ricoeur: An Anthology of his Work*, ed. Charles E. Reagan
& David Stewart (Boston: Beacon Press, 1978), pp. 161.

30. Ricoeur, *OA*, p. 143.

31. Ricoeur, "Life in Quest of Narrative," p. 32.

32. The historian Hayden White describes the plot as "a
structure of relationships by which the events contained in
the account are endowed with a meaning by being identified
as parts of an integrated whole" (Hayden White, *The Content
of the Form*, p. 9).

33. Ricoeur, *OA*, p. 142.

34. Ibid.

35. Ricoeur, "Explanation and Understanding: On Some
Remarkable Connections Among the Theory of the Text,
Theory of Action, and Theory of History," p. 165.

36. Ricoeur, *OA*, p. 161.

37. Ricoeur, "Life in Quest of Narrative," p. 33.

38. Alasdair MacIntyre, *After Virtue: a Study in Moral
Theory* (Notre Dame: University of Notre Dame Press, 1981),
pp. 218-19.

39. Ricoeur, *TN3*, pp. 248-49.

40. Ricoeur, "Life in Quest of Narrative," pp. 32-33.

41. Ricoeur, *OA*, p. 143.

42. Ricoeur, *OA*, pp. 125-26.

43. Ricoeur divides *OA* into ten studies as opposed to

chapters, thereby flagging that his book is to be viewed as a collection of essays rather than a sustained argument (see Introduction of *OA*).

44. Another case that raises doubts about survival is the thought experiment where Parfit imagines that each half of his brain is successfully transplanted into the similar bodies of his two brothers.

> There will be two future people, each of whom will have the body of one of my brothers, and will be fully psychologically continuous with me, because he has half of my brain. Knowing this, we know everything. I may ask, "But shall I be one of these two people, or the other, or neither?" But I should regard this as an empty question (Derek Parfit, *Reasons and Persons* [Oxford: Oxford University Press, 1984], p. 260).

Parfit is saying that he will not live as Parfit, but neither does he die.

45. Parfit, *Reasons and Persons,* pp. 199–201.

46. Ricoeur, *OA*, p. 135.

47. By "empty" he means that they do not refer to a range of possibilities any of which might be true, but one of which must be true. An alternative meaning, Parfit mentions in passing, is one where a question is considered empty because it has no answer, or any answer we might give it would be arbitrary (Parfit, *Reasons and Persons,* p. 260).

48. Ricoeur cites Woolf's *Mrs. Dalloway* as an example of the way Woolf experiments with the "subtle variations between the time of consciousness and chronological time" (Ricoeur, *TN* 1, pp. 101–12; Virginia Woolf, *Mrs. Dalloway* [San Diego, CA: Harcourt Inc., 1981]).

49. Aristotle, "Categories," in *The Complete Works of Aris-*

totle 1, Bollingen Series LXXI, ed. Jonathan Barnes (Princeton, NJ: Princeton University Press, 1984), 6 1450a 25–1450b 1.

50. Ricoeur, "Narrative Identity," p. 78.

52. Ricoeur, *OA*, pp. 149–50.

53. For example, Dennett, *CE*; Sigmund Freud, "Remembering, Repeating and Working-Through," in *Standard Edition of the Complete Psychological Works of Sigmund Freud* XII, ed. James Strachey in collaboration with Anna Freud (London: Hogarth Press, 1964), pp. 147–56; Michel Foucault, "Technologies of the Self," in *Technologies of the Self*, ed. Luther H. Martin, Huck Gutman, and Patrick H. Hutton (London: Tavistock Publications, 1988); Ulric Neisser and Robyn Fivush, eds., *The Remembering Self, Construction and Accuracy in the Self-Narrative* (Cambridge: Cambridge University Press, 1994).

54. Ricoeur, "Narrative Identity," pp. 78–79. He puts it even more strongly in *OA*: "The Earth here is something different, and something more, than a planet: it is the mythical name of our corporeal anchoring in the world" (p. 150).

55. Ricoeur, "Narrative Identity," p. 80.

56. Ricoeur, *OA*, p. 135.

57. Paul Ricoeur, "From Metaphysics to Moral Philosophy," *Philosophy Today* 39, no. 4 (1996): 454.

58. Ricoeur, *OA*, p. 302.

59. Paul Ricoeur, *Freud and Philosophy: An Essay on Interpretation* and *Hermeneutics and the Human Sciences*, ed. and trans. John B. Thompson (Cambridge: Cambridge University Press, 1981). Of particular interest in this regard is Ricoeur's essay, "The Question of Proof in Freud's Writings," in *Hermeneutics and the Human Sciences*, pp. 247–73.

60. Paul Ricoeur, "Reply to G. B. Madison," in *The Philosophy of Paul Ricoeur*, ed. Lewis Edwin Hahn (Chicago and La Salle, Illinois: Open Court, 1995), p. 93.

61. Ricoeur has no difficulty acknowledging that any philo-

sophical enquiry aims at coherence and must presuppose some ground or set of principles: "All philosophical discourse aiming at coherence seems to me to include principles that some take as derived and others as primitive or 'grounding' at least for the particular discourse under consideration" (Ricoeur, "From Metaphysics to Moral Philosophy," p. 445).

62. Ricoeur, *OA*, p. 302.

63. Paul Ricoeur, *History and Truth*, trans. Charles A. Kelbley (Evanston: Northwestern University Press, 1965), p. 96. Originally published as *Histoire et vérité* (Paris: Seuil, 1955).

64. Ricoeur, *OA*, p. 302.

65. Ibid., pp. 15–21.

66. René Descartes, *Oeuvres de Descartes* 4, 11 vols., trans. Charles Adam and Paul Tannery (Paris: Vrin, 1964–1974), pp. 9, 16.

67. Friedrich W. Nietzsche, *Will to Power* 15 in *Complete Works*, trans. Anthony M. Ludovici (Edinburgh: T. N. Fowlis, 1910), p. 7; cited in Ricoeur, *OA,* p. 13 fn.19.

68. Nietzsche, *Will to Power*, p. 7; cited in Ricoeur, *OA*, p. 14.

69. Ricoeur, *OA*, p. 21.

70. Ricoeur in Changeux and Ricoeur, *What Makes Us Think?* p. 16.

71. Ibid., p. 102.

72. Ricoeur, *OA*, p. 21.

73. Ricoeur, "From Metaphysics to Moral Philosophy," pp. 453–54. Ricoeur describes a Hegelian conscience as a "'spirit certain of itself' over every moral vision of the world, at that stage where the active and the judging consciousness, confessing the limit of their respective points of view, and renouncing their respective partiality, mutually recognize and absolve each other" (ibid). Ricoeur also draws on two notions from Heidegger: "the idea of an uprooting of the self from the

anonymity of the 'they' as well as the idea of an appeal that Dasein addresses to itself from the depths of itself, but also higher than itself" (ibid).

74. Ibid., p. 454.

75. Ricoeur, *OA*, pp. 22–23.

76. Ricoeur, "From Metaphysics to Moral Philosophy," p. 454.

77. Ricoeur, *OA*, p. 73.

78. Ricoeur, "From Metaphysics to Moral Philosophy," p. 455.

79. Ricoeur, *OA*, p. 22.

Chapter Six

NARRATIVE ATTESTATION

Ricoeur's interpretation of the Aristotelian notion of emplotment casts the plot as a source of the identity of the capable self. On this view, the journey of any individual life provides a horizon of possibilities that are mediated through available cultural and literary genres defining what a good journey is and what it takes to be heroic, stoic, or suave. These genres provide the living human individual with models of "everyman"—universal characters whose lives are cloths out of which particular stories are woven. Different genres offer diverse narrative possibilities: some stories have stable characters with conventional plots—beginnings, middles, and ends—others hardly count as stories at all, with unstable characters and surprise beginnings and endings. Moreover, the implications of the events of any story are open to a number of readings by possible readers who will view some actions as purposive and others as random. In this way, "[i]n place of an *ego* enamoured of itself arises a *self* instructed by cultural symbols, the first among which are the narratives handed down in our literary tradition. And these narratives give us a unity which is not substantial but narrative."[1]

The critical question with regard to this position concerns how these different narrative unities are to be evaluated. On the one hand, as I indicated in the last chapter, Ricoeur opposes the notion of attestational certainty to other traditional standards of truth. On the other hand, as discussed in chapter 4, one of the concerns Ricoeur has with Heideggerian hermeneutics is that it does not provide a means of deciding between rival accounts of the world. Granted that Ricoeur eschews both the threatened relativism of the Heideggerian stance as well as certainties claimed by other positions, his solution to the problem of deciding among rival interpretations of an individual's life is *narrative attestation*.[2]

Narrative attestation describes the level of certainty one can have about the narrative self. It is achieved on the basis of appeal to literary and psychoanalytic standards of excellence, which help to decide among conflicting accounts of the narrative self. The first challenge that must be met in this regard is to examine the intimate relationship that exists between literature and the imagination. To the extent that literary accounts of human life, including biography and autobiography, are woven by the imagination, the question arises as to how conflicting stories might be adjudicated. The first question is: Are there any "facts" outside of the text that can be appealed to in order to settle interpretative disagreements? And the second is: If there are no neutral facts, will any "tall tale" meet the requirements of narrative attestation?

FACT AND FICTION

A contested area between literature and life that Ricoeur explores in his three volume project, *Time and Narrative* (*TN*), is presented through a detailed examination of the relationship between literary and historical theory.[3] A core aim of this project is to reframe the traditional opposition between history as a factual discourse and literature as a fictional discourse. In it, Ricoeur draws from a wide range of sources to argue that history and literature cannot be radically separated, because even though their content may *appear* to differ—fact and fiction—both "historical events" and "literary events" are narratively constructed. Moreover, he argues that both discourses are successful in so far as they reveal or disclose through this narrative form a fundamental structure of human existence: temporality.

In essence, Ricoeur's argument is that events in history are not "mere facts" that are subsequently distorted by narrative construction—these events are already understood through the detour of cultural and historical interpretation. The historical theorist, Hayden White, who adopts a position similar to Ricoeur's, defends the role of historical narrative and makes the point in the following way:

> The contention is not that historians impose a narrative form on sets or sequences of real events that might just as legitimately be represented in some other, non-narrative discourse but that historical events possess the same structure as narrative discourse. It is their narrative structure that distinguishes

historical events from natural events (which lack such a structure). It is because historical events possess a narrative structure that historians are justified in regarding stories as valid representations of such events and treating such representations as explanations of them.[4]

Ricoeur claims the reason narrative emplotment can be so easily mapped on to individual human lives is because the temporal nature of human life provides an order upon which the structure of the narrative can adhere. In sum, the temporal nature of human experience and action encourages the structuring of these "interpretations" in narrative terms. For example, the concepts of action specify "order," "progression," "direction," "purpose," and "goal." He describes human life as a "story in its nascent state," and an "activity and a passion in search of a narrative."[5] Where an uninterpreted life is merely a biological phenomenon, the structure of human action and suffering is already plot-like, and this distinguishes it from the movement and psychophysiological behavior of animal and mineral life.

The individual can be said to be "tangled up in stories" which happen to him before any story is recounted. This entanglement then appears as the prehistory of the story told, the beginning of which is chosen by the narrator. The pre-history of the story is what connects it up to a vaster whole and gives it a background. This background is made up of the living imbrication of all lived stories. The stories that are told must then be made to emerge out of this back-

ground. And as they emerge, the implied subject also
emerges. We can then say: the story answers to the
man. The main consequence of this existential
analysis of man as being entangled in stories is that
narrating is a secondary process grafted on our "being
entangled in stories." Recounting, following, understanding stories is then simply the continuation of
these unspoken stories.[6]

He deploys a much elaborated version of the Aristotelian
concept of *mimesis*, or imitation, to express his view that
narratives neither mirror nor falsify life, but that human
lives are already "tangled up in stories." Understanding
mimesis as "prefiguration," he claims that everyday
events have a symbolic character (for example, activities
such as shopping or banking are already ritualized; they
already contain an "inchoate narrativity" or "prenarrative
structure").[7] In this way, narrative is not grafted on; it
already prefigures in human activities. The core of
Ricoeur's argument is precisely this: the polarization
between living and telling is exaggerated because human
lives lend themselves to being told as a story. While there
are facts such as birth and death, individual capacities
and conditions that escape narrative control, narration is
in some sense integral to human life. In a sense, human
lives are "naturally" narrative lives.

My basic hypothesis . . . is the following: the common
feature of human experience, that which is marked,
organized and clarified by the fact of storytelling in all
its forms, is its temporal character. Everything that is
recounted occurs in time, takes time, unfolds tempo-

rally; and what unfolds in time can be recounted. Perhaps, indeed, every temporal process is recognized as such only to the extent that it can, in one way or another, be recounted. This reciprocity which is assumed to exist between narrativity and temporality is the theme of my present research.[8]

This position can be opposed to the more usual view of the relationship between narrative and real life which holds that the latter does not have the same character as the former.[9] On the standard view, real life affords mere sequences of events, and narratives are considered to be fictional, not just because they relate events that never happened, but because they relate events through a particular form. It follows that biography, documentary, history, and discourses that claim to talk of real events actually impose on reality because they present events in narrative form and thus distort them. The narrative theorist, David Carr, summarizes this view: "At best [narrative] constitutes an escape, a consolation, at worst an opiate, either as self-delusion or . . . imposed from without by some authoritative narrative voice in the interest of manipulation and power. In either case it is an act of violence, a betrayal, an imposition on reality or life and on ourselves."[10]

What further distinguishes Ricoeur's account of narrative from such a view is his claim that narrative transforms rather than distorts real life. Understanding mimesis as "refiguration," narratives, according to Ricoeur, involve both revelation and transformation.[11] He compares the unifying capacity of the narrative with the unifying capacity of the metaphor. In both cases, something "new," the "as yet unsaid" is brought into being:

With narrative, the semantic innovation lies in the inventing of another work of synthesis—a plot. By means of the plot, goals, causes, and chance are brought together within the temporal unity of a whole and complete action. It is this synthesis of the heterogeneous that brings narrative close to metaphor. In both cases, the new thing—the as yet unsaid, the unwritten—springs up in language. Here a living metaphor, that is, a new pertinence in the predication, there a feigned plot, that is, a new congruence in the organization of events.[12]

Ricoeur claims that an individual's life is narratively unified on the basis of an unstable "mixture" between "fabulation" and "actual experience."

As for the notion of the narrative unity of a life, it must be seen as an unstable mixture of fabulation and actual experience. It is precisely because of the elusive character of real life that we need the help of fiction to organize life retrospectively, after the fact, prepared to take as provisional and open to revision any figure of emplotment borrowed from fiction or from history.[13]

The narrative "refiguring" of reality is a two-fold action; it both uncovers and transforms the meaning of events in human lives.

[M]etaphorical and narrative statements, taken in hand by reading, aim at refiguring reality, in the twofold sense of *uncovering* the concealed dimensions of human experience and of *transforming* our vision of the world ... refiguration seemed to me ... to constitute an active reorganization of our being-in-the-world, performed by the reader following the invitation of the text, citing Proust once again, to become the reader of oneself.[14]

What Ricoeur insists upon is the importance of both documentary history—the counting of bodies in the death camps—as well as the more enriched recounting of what these deaths mean, to their fellow prisoners and to contemporary analysts:

> This is not to ignore the fact that sometimes fictions come closer to what really happened than do mere historical narratives, where fictions go directly to the *meaning* beyond or beneath the facts. It is puzzling. But, finally, we have to return to a body count. You have to accurately *count* the corpses in the death camps as well as offering vivid narrative *accounts* that people will remember.[15]

On a close reading of these passages, an objection could be made that Ricoeur is not the thorough-going hermeneutic philosopher that his billing in the tradition indicates. For example, when he delineates the "narrative unity of a life" as a mixture of "fabulation" and "actual experience," he implies that a distinction can clearly made between fabulation on the one hand and experience on the other.[16] Furthermore, he admits that "finally, we have to return to a body count. You have to accurately *count* the corpses in the death camps." This implies that Ricoeur's hermeneutic stance must ultimately face up to the facts of the matter and be tested by them. On this view, it is no more, nor less, than a sophisticated realist position with a coherence theory of truth.

On the other hand, Ricoeur argues we must not "ignore the fact that sometimes fictions come closer to what really happened," because they go directly to the "meaning *beyond or beneath the facts*." The idea here is that we must not privilege the supposed neutrality of facts over their significance to someone. Granted then that these passages are ambiguous and confusing, they can be read in a way that underlines rather than undermines Ricoeur's overall position. I understand him to claim that facts are important—that accurately counting the number of dead people in the Nazi death camps is important—but that what is at stake in such accuracy is the significance it has for different people. Such a reading would take it that the facts speak only within an interpretative framework—so much so, for example, that the significance of "ten dead bodies" is only made fully intelligible when it is filled out as "ten dead Jews," "ten dead lesbians," "ten dead children," "ten dead mothers," "ten dead murderers," "ten dead foetuses," "ten dead Americans," "ten dead Iraqis," "ten dead rapists," or "ten dead dolphins." (And these categories—Jews, lesbians, children, etc.— are, in turn, constituted by cultural and political interpretative frameworks.)

One powerful testament to the salience of Ricoeur's analysis of the relationship between fiction and history is Richard White's book, *Remembering Ahanagran: Storytelling in a Family's Past*. In his fascinating account of his mother's life, White takes the stories that were told to him by his mother—about her girlhood in Co. Kerry, Ireland, emigration to the United States, and early adult years in Chicago—and he compares them with the other traces of his mother's life that he, as a historian, researches (for example, other witnesses, newspaper clippings, publicly recorded events, archives, and court records). What White finds is that his mother's stories do not always match the documented evidence that he unearths; for example, his mother, Sara, recounts how she vividly remembers witnessing her own mother being violently assaulted by British government troops during the "Time of the Troubles," while in fact White discovers that Sara was only one year old when the incident occurred and so is remembering only what she heard about from others. However, White does not conclude from this that history is truthful and Sara's stories are mere fabulation. He describes his book as a "dangerous conversation" with memory: an "anti-memoir," not because it attacks memory, but rather because it questions memory and is, in turn, challenged by it.[17]

> My mother, Sara, like all of us, has constructed versions of the past. She has made memories where I seek history. It would be mean-spirited, trivial, and despicable wilfully to destroy the memories of one you love. That my mother's memories are not a literal rendering of the past, not a transparent window on her experiences, is the beginning of this book not its end. I am interested in what my mother's memories are, not what they are not. They are creations; they are a making sense; they are a conscious rewriting in the light of the person she has become and continues to become. My history needs to understand such memo-

ries, and other constructions of the past as well. History cannot afford to dismiss its rivals as simply fabricated or false, or history will weaken its own ability to understand the strange worlds we live in. . . . I imagine a past in which some truth lies. This past is a place that yields a dense, almost impenetrable, imaginative growth. Historians can only hope to tap this fertility and trim and discipline what grows so luxuriantly. Beyond history's garden gates, the thick jungle of the past remains, and memory's trails lead off into it.[18]

What is important for White, and also what I believe is at stake for Ricoeur, is the idea that what is related through story-telling cannot be exhausted by being reduced to a supposedly neutral set of facts. Even if we were to allow that historical documentation is nothing over and above a literal translation of human events, it would still be the case that telling the story of these events captures and communicates additional truths that are lost on supposedly pure historical renderings.

What is also at stake for Ricoeur in this regard is his view that facts cannot be separated out from the discourse in which they are articulated, be it history or fiction. This means that, for him, one investigates personal narratives of human action, not simply in order to ascertain whether or not they took place—their real or imaginary status—but to assess their meaning, positive or negative, for any given interpreter. It is a complex intelligibility or understanding of the self and of human possibilities that he is looking for, not (supposedly) bare knowledge: "a) knowledge of the self is an interpretation; b) the interpretation of the self, in turn, finds narrative,

among other signs and symbols, to be a privileged mediation; c) this mediation borrows from history as much as
fiction making the life story a fictive history or, if you
prefer, an historical fiction."[19]

NARRATIVE ATTESTATION

Narrative Intelligibility

Granted that Ricoeur's account of *mimesis* undermines
the traditional opposition between fact and fiction, it follows that there is no obvious way of deciding between
conflicting narrative accounts of human lives. The question that arises then is whether or not Ricoeur's
hermeneutic detour leads us to the Dennettian *cul de
sac*, outlined in chapter 3. There, I concluded that
Daniel Dennett's naturalist account of the fictional self as
a center of narrative gravity was epistemologically fragile
because there was no way of determining the conditions
of self-persistence because of the gappiness of consciousness and, by implication, memory.

Like Dennett, Ricoeur also acknowledges that there is
a gap between narrative unity and the temporal unity of
human life. In *TN*3, for example, he dismisses the possibility of unifying the self on the basis of the Husserlian
account of the human experience of time. Husserl's
thesis is that while we may be able to imagine the passage of time as a linear sequence of isolated occurrences,
we nevertheless, as human beings, experience these
occurrences as informed and weighted by memories of

the past and anticipation of the future.[20] However valuable an insight this may be into human experience in general, such an extension of the present into the past and the future is too fragmented according to Ricoeur and does not provide the kind of continuity of consciousness that would form the basis of a perduring self: "The major discovery with which we have credited Husserl, the constitution of the extended present by the continuous addition of retentions and protentions to the source-point of the living present, only partially answers this question. . . . I do not see how retentions of retentions can make up a single flux."[21] The problem for Ricoeur is that memory is too unstable and fragile to provide an undisputed link with the past.

However, where Dennett's account of the discontinuity of consciousness leads him to conclude that the self is temporally unstable; Ricoeur's hermeneutic alternative, which equally acknowledges that consciousness is discontinuous, nevertheless suggests alternative ways of construing the self as a narrative unity and alternative strategies for deciding among different narrative accounts. As outlined in chapter 5, his contention that narrative identity invokes identity conditions of selfhood, not sameness, his rejection of the Cartesian and naturalist standards of certainty in respect of their modes of verification and validation, and his careful delineation of a hermeneutic mode of understanding and an attested order of truth make this possible. For Ricoeur, any given life-story can be evaluated or attested on the basis of its capacity to provide unity for the individual whose life is thus recounted. Such a unity must meet certain standards of narrative intelligibility, and these are set by culturally available models of heroism and story-telling practices.

> It comes to terms with the general condition of acceptability that we apply when we read any story, be it historical or fictional. In the terms of W. B. Gallie, a story has to be "followable," and in this sense, "self-explanatory." We interpolate explanation when the narrative process is blocked and in order to "follow-further." These explanations are acceptable to the extent that they may be grafted upon the archetypes of storytelling which have been culturally developed and which rule our actual competence to follow new stories.[22]

For Ricoeur, there is an "intuitive preunderstanding" that human lives are "more readable when they have been interpreted in terms of the stories that people tell about them," and, in turn, that these life stories are "more intelligible when the narrative models of plots—borrowed from history or from fiction (drama or novel)—are applied to them."[23] Ricoeur's privileging of the Aristotelian idea of emplotment offers one model of narrative intelligibility which requires that actions, thoughts, and feelings are seen to follow one another in a plausible (though not necessarily predictable) way. Such a coherence rests on a special kind of logical relationship among narrative events that pertains because of the beginning-middle-end form of the narrative.

> To follow a history, [or narrative] in fact, is to understand a succession of actions, of thoughts, of feelings

presenting at the same time a certain direction, but also some surprises (coincidences, recognitions, revelations, etc.). Consequently, the conclusion of the history is never deducible and predictable. That is why it is necessary to follow the development. But neither can the history be disconnected: even though not deducible, its ending must be plausible. Thus, in every retold history there is a bond of logical continuity that is completely specific, because the outcome must at the same time be contingent and plausible. . . . To follow a history is a completely specific activity by which we continuously anticipate a final course and an outcome, and we successively correct our expectations until they coincide with the actual outcome. Then we say we have understood.[24]

In addition, the coherent life story is one where discord has been reduced, where connections have been forged between disparate events and random incidents and contingencies. Granted these requirements of narrative intelligibility, Ricoeur's account of the self is not produced by an unreigned imagination where any possible story can be told.[25]

Psychoanalytic intelligibility

Ricoeur also flags a detour through the discourse of psychoanalysis in order to throw additional light on what is involved in narrative attestation. He suggests that the case histories of psychoanalysis provide a "particularly instructive laboratory" for a philosophical inquiry into the notion of narrative identity.[26] What is at stake here is the claim that if the processes of narration and the processes of psychoanalysis are significantly equivalent, then the validation criteria for one may be applicable to the other. In other words, we can consider any narrative account of the self "attested" if it comes at the end of a process that is similar to the psychoanalytic process.

Specifically, he identifies a feature of psychoanalysis that he thinks is also central to narrativity. This feature relates to one of the objectives of psychoanalysis, which is to "substitute for the bits and pieces of stories that are unintelligible as well as unbearable, a coherent and acceptable story."[27] It involves the analytic process hereafter translated as "working-through."[28] I will examine the latter below. First, I want to delineate the grounds on which Ricoeur distinguishes the function of psychoanalytic theories from other empirical theories. This distinction is important because it can also be read as an indication of the ways in which narrative theory must also be distinguished from empirical theory.

Ricoeur has written several essays that distinguish psychoanalysis from scientific psychology and posit the project of psychoanalysis in terms of a phenomenological hermeneutical enquiry.[29] Responding to the general positivist criticism that psychoanalytic theory does not satisfy even the minimal requirements of a scientific theory, Ricoeur's claim in *Freud and Philosophy* is that "psychoanalysis is not a science of observation; it is an interpretation, more comparable to history than to psychology."[30] Specifically, it has been objected that psychoanalytic theory does not readily satisfy two key criteria that are applied to the empirical sciences: verification and validation.[31] First, the empirical verification of any theory presupposes that its concepts can be related in some law-like or rule-bound way with some definite set of facts. Further, that it is possible to deduce some definite consequences or implications from them. In the case of psychoanalysis, Ricoeur acknowledges that "the energy notions of Freudian theory are so vague and metaphorical that it seems impossible to deduce from them any determinate conclusions ... further, any coordination with facts of behavior is clouded over with an invincible ambiguity."[32] In sum, psychoanalytic terms do not behave in a law-like way, are vague and seemingly unrelated to facts, and fail to predict behavior.

Second, it is argued that empirical validation presupposes that some conditions can be identified in order to determine whether or not any claim is valid and, moreover, that objective procedures are available to adjudicate among rival claims and verify the predictions of any theory. Again, in the case of psychoanalysis, there is the problem of identifying what might satisfy the requirements of validity: Is a psychoanalytic claim proven because the client finds it coherent, or because her condition improves? The criterion of therapeutic success cannot be used as a means of assessment of rival interpretations, because the rates of improvement brought about by the therapeutic process cannot be easily separated from improvements that may happen independently and spontaneously. Moreover, because of the specific relationship between the analysand and the analyst, a number of independent observers cannot have access to the same data—objective evaluation is impossible.

Indeed, Ricoeur acknowledges, "one cannot dispel the suspicion that interpretations are forced upon the data by the interpreter."[33] Given the difficulties with the usual criteria of verification and validation, Ricoeur concludes that psychoanalysis is not empirical; it is interpretive.

> For the analyst, therefore, behavior is not a dependent variable observable from without, but is rather the expression of changes of meaning of the subject's history, as they are revealed in the analytical situation. . . . They [the facts of behavior] do not function as observables, but as signifiers (significants) for history of desire.[34]

In this passage, Ricoeur indicates that psychoanalysis does not function in the way that empirical sciences do because its objects of analysis—desires—are mediated through behavior which must be interpreted not by any possible observer, but within the specific analytical situation.

Strong comparisons can be made between narrative accounts of the self and psychoanalytic accounts of the psyche. Just as psychoanalytic theory cannot be verified because there are no definite facts related in a law-like fashion to its concepts, so the factual events that occur chronologically in the life of any individual do not have a law-like relation to the narrative accounts in which they may or may not feature. Equally, because the relationship between events and narrative is ambiguous and revisable, narrative accounts are unreliable predictors of an individual's future behavior. In addition, empirical validation presupposes that sets of claims can be tested in some way and that objective procedures are available to adjudicate between rival claims. However, narrative accounts are not straightforwardly testable, and there seems to be no reason why third-person accounts of a person's life should be any more accurate than first-person accounts. Indeed, first-person narrative accounts may have access to information that is unavailable to independent observers. Given these difficulties, narrative intelligibility is clearly of an interpretative, not an empirical kind. It does not function in the way that the empirical sciences do because its objects of interpretation— motivations, desires, intentions, and events—are mediated in terms of a particular historical and cultural understanding and within the context of a single, unique and unrepeatable life.

On the positive side, Ricoeur claims that psychoanalysis does have a function that is proper to it. In "The Question of Proof in Freud's Writings," he develops this theme with his thesis that psychoanalytic theory codifies what happens in the psychoanalytic situation/relationship. It is the psychoanalytic relationship that is the source of the "facts" that theory must select and analyze. Ricoeur argues that psychoanalytic facts have a fourfold nature. They must be articulable, intersubjectively accessible, fantasized, and recounted. These four criteria serve to identify the domain or selection of facts which psychoanalytic theory takes into account. My interest lies in the fourth criterion, because it is here that narrative theory and psychoanalytic theory most directly overlap. First of all, however, I will briefly summarize the other three.

Ricoeur's first criterion of the psychoanalytic situation excludes *what cannot be articulated* from the field of psychoanalytical investigation. Its focus is solely on what he calls the "semantic dimension of desire," or that part of experience capable of "*being said*."[35] This restriction of language "forces desire to speak, to pass through the defile of words, excluding substitute satisfactions as well as any regression toward acting out."[36] Facts in psychoanalysis are not facts of observable behavior, but reports of dreams and symptoms that, even if partially observable, enter the field of analysis only in relation to other elements already reported. Thus, the task of psychoanalytic investigation is not to establish facts, but to interpret the meaning and motivation behind reports.

The second criterion of the psychoanalytic situation is that it selects not only what is capable of articulation, but also what can be articulated to another person; it is intersubjective. Ricoeur sees an important role in the process of transference whereby the analyst can halt any resistance to remembering that the analysand may have by providing a "playground," so to speak, wherein the analysand may explore the fulfillment or denial of her desires by projecting them onto the analyst.[37]

The third criterion is related to the ways in which the unconscious expresses itself, specifically to the coherence of what Freud called "psychical reality," in order to distinguish it from material reality. The famous example of this is Freud's claim that, from a clinical point of view, the truth or falsity of reports of infantile scenes of child abuse is not completely relevant (though, presumably, it is profoundly important on other grounds, personal and social). What this means for Ricoeur is that "the criterion for this reality is no longer that it is observable, but that it presents a coherence and a resistance comparable to that of material reality."[38]

> He [Freud] then goes on to refer to infantile scenes which themselves "are not always true." This is an especially important admission when we remember how difficult it was for Freud to give up his initial hypothesis of the father's real seduction of the child. More than fifteen years later he remarked how disturbing this discovery remained for him. What is so disturbing about it? Precisely that it is not clinically relevant whether the infantile scenes are true or false. And it does not matter, therefore, from an epistemological point of view either. This is what is expressed by the phrase "psychical reality."[39]

In what ways might "psychical reality" present a kind of coherence that is similar to what happens in the real world? Ricoeur argues that childhood recollections, whether based in real life or not, present an organized structure, are limited in number, and typify the experiences of many. Other psychic phenomena such as dreams display a thematic unity so that they can easily be substituted for one another. What is consistent about many dreams, no matter how diverse, is their meaning; their "[r]eality is their meaning."[40]

Memory as Work

Ricoeur designates narrativity as a fourth criterion of selection in the psychoanalytic situation because he views case histories as the primary texts of psychoanalysis.

These cases represent whatever is capable of narrative construction from the client's experiences. While Freud does not refer to the narrative character of psychoanalytic experience directly, Ricoeur claims that it is implicit in Freud's treatment of memory. For Freud, the process of remembering involves the overcoming of resistance, and Ricoeur views this as, essentially, a narrative act.

> But what is it to remember? It is not just to recall certain isolated events, but to become capable of forming meaningful sequences and ordered connections. In short, it is to be able to constitute one's own existence in the form of a story where a memory as such is only a fragment of the story. It is the narrative structure of such life stories that makes a case history.[41]

Ricoeur distinguishes the notion of "memory as work" from a notion of memory that simply extends the act of perception into the past (the latter seems to be the understanding of memory adopted by Dennett).[42] This notion of memory as work extends the sense of memory beyond simply a cognitive operation, to an intersubjective operation that is also embodied in habits, routines, and gestures. It also counteracts Ricoeur's earlier worries about the instability and fragility of memory mentioned in relation to Husserl. This Freudian notion of remembering involves a reconstruction and rehabilitation of meaning:

> Here we see that we are far removed from the notion of a memory, which would simply reproduce real events in a sort of perception of the past; this is

instead a work that goes over and over extremely complex structuralizations. It is this work of memory that is implied, among other things, by the notion of the story or narrative structure of existence. [43]

Referring to Freud's essay, "Remembering, Repetition, and Working-Through," Ricoeur describes how Freud is concerned with moments in the process of psychoanalytic cure, where the client simply repeats symptoms and is prevented thereby from recollecting or reconstructing a past that is acceptable or understandable to her. For Freud, both analyst and client must have patience and accept that they cannot go directly to the truth, and he objects to those techniques such as hypnotic treatment, which view the act of remembering in a very simple way. In standard hypnosis, clients simply place themselves in the earlier situation, never confuse it with the present one, and give an account of their mental states adding what they can, transforming unconscious processes into conscious ones. Many cases, however, do not behave so smoothly. Often, according to Freud, the client does not "*remember* anything of what he has forgotten and repressed, but *acts* it out. He reproduces it not as a memory but as an action; he *repeats* it, without, of course, knowing that he is repeating it."[44] One example Freud gives is of a client who does not remember that he defied parental authority. Instead, he behaves defiantly toward the analyst. In another, the client does not remember experiencing childhood shame around sexual activity, but declares that he is ashamed of the fact that he is now undergoing treatment. Repeating is the client's way of remembering: "The greater the resistance, the more extensively will acting out (repetition) replace remembering."[45] Freud recommends that the new task of the psychoanalyst is to be prepared for struggle:

> He is prepared for a perpetual struggle with his patient to keep in the psychical sphere all the impulses which the patient would like to direct into the motor sphere; and he celebrates it as a triumph for the treatment if he can bring it about that something that the patient wishes to discharge in action is disposed of through the work of remembering.[46]

So the therapeutic task is not for the analyst to simply uncover resistances and point them out. This is because the process of naming resistances does not mean they will be halted. The analytic situation requires a "working-through" of these resistances.

> The analyst had merely forgotten that giving the resistance a name could not result in its immediate cessation. One must allow the patient time to become more conversant with this resistance with which he has now become acquainted, to *work through* it, to overcome it, by continuing, in defiance of it, the analytic work according to the fundamental rule of analysis. . . . This working-through of the resistances may in practice turn out to be an arduous task for the subject of the analysis and a trial of patience for the analyst.[47]

The benefit of the Freudian account of memory as work for Ricoeur's account of narrative attestation is that it provides criteria for the reliability of particular narrative interpretations of the self. The process of "working-through" demonstrates for Freud that the history of the analysand is not linear in the sense that the past dictates what happens in the present. Rather, it is the analytic work of the present that permits her to recover from and rehabilitate traumatic events from the past. In this way, "working-through" invokes the aspect of narrative emplotment that eschews chronological ordering in favor of narrative coherence. Moreover, any adequate narrative self on this account must be a self that is determined only after a struggle of self-examination:

> This connection between self-constancy and narrative identity confirms one of my oldest convictions, namely, that the self of self-knowledge is not the egotistical and narcissistic ego whose hypocrisy and naiveté the hermeneutics of suspicion have denounced, along with its aspects of an ideological superstructure and infantile and neurotic archaism. The self of self-knowledge is the fruit of an examined life, to recall Socrates' phrase in the Apology. And an examined life is, in large part, one purged, one clarified by the cathartic effects of the narratives, be they historical or fictional, conveyed by our culture. So self-constancy refers to a self instructed by the works of a culture that it has applied to itself.[48]

What distinguishes narrative recounting from other forms of self-knowledge is that the form of narrative recounting itself is a particular mode of self-examination in terms of which one can achieve different levels of competence. For example, when Ricoeur considers the imaginary flights of fictional characters, Don Quixote and Madame Bovary, he indicates that they are self-deceived on two different levels.[49] Explicitly, he claims that a "naïve conception" of *mimesis* would deem them self-deceived because they imagine that they themselves are the fictional characters they have read about. However, what is implicit in his remarks is that on his more sophisticated deployment of *mimesis*, Madame Bovary and Don Quixote are self-deceived, not just because they imitate imaginary characters, but because they are not sufficiently self-examined. What they lack is the narrative competence to treat their own lives as histories with narrative coherence. Such coherence is achievable through a process of education that involves not the retelling and revising of one's biography in the light of documentary evidence alone, but also being open to the way one's story might be cast by others—recovering, revising, and assuming responsibility for what has been repressed. "In this respect, one can speak of education to narrative coherence, of education to narrative identity. One can learn to tell the same story otherwise, learn to let it be told by others than oneself, learn to submit the narrative of one's life to the critique of documentary history."[50]

This level of narrative intelligibility is expressed through Ricoeur's claim that narrative recounting is a task of "recognizing oneself":

> We may even say, then, that the patient is both the actor
> and the critic of a history which he is at first unable to
> recount. The problem of *recognising oneself* is the

problem of recovering the ability to recount one's own history, to continue endlessly to give the form of a story to reflections on oneself. And working-through is nothing other than this continuous narration.[51]

Usually, the term "recognition" invokes the idea that one "knows again" oneself or others, and if it is understood in this way, Ricoeur's argument is circular, because it claims that the self already knows itself—the self is presupposed. However, at the cost of confusion perhaps, but not circularity, Ricoeur defines recognition as the ability to recount through emplotment and reflection. In doing so, he stresses that remembering one's past involves an intersubjective reconstruction and rehabilitation of experiences, in the light of available stories of heroic and villainous characters, into a story of oneself.

This narrative interpretation of psychoanalytic theory implies that the story of a life grows out of stories that have not been recounted and that have been repressed in the direction of actual stories which the subject could take charge of and consider to be constitutive of his personal identity. It is the quest of personal identity which assures the continuity between the potential or virtual story and the explicit story for which we assume responsibility.[52]

Ricoeur's thesis—that narration is one of a number of unifying human activities on the basis of which an individual can attest that they are a persisting self—provides a rich and thought-provoking alternative to either Cartesian accounts of a substantial self or naturalist accounts of a fictional self. Such an identity is possible because, from Ricoeur's phenomenological point of view, humans are essentially temporal beings, and the appeal of the narrative form is that it represents this feature in a particular way. Further, any account of the narrative self can be attested in terms of the standards and norms of narrative intelligibility, and, again, these radically differ from the standards and norms of rational or empirical explanation because they are drawn from the laboratories of literature and psychoanalysis.

In sum, narrative standards of intelligibility evaluate conflicting narratives of the self on the basis of the story's followability (the non-chronological, but nevertheless, logical succession of actions, thoughts, and feelings); emotional depth and communicability; the willingness of an individual to recognize herself or himself in the terms of a particular story and assume responsibility for it; the degree of subjective and inter-subjective credibility of a story; and the level of self-examination involved.

NOTES TO CHAPTER 6

1. Ricoeur, "Life in Quest of Narrative," p. 33.

2. Ricoeur, himself, does not use the term "narrative attestation." I borrow it from Jean Greisch who uses it to emphasize what he and I both see as the strong bond between the concept of narrative identity and the phenomenon of attestation. See Jean Greisch, "Testimony and Attestation," in *Paul Ricoeur, The Hermeneutics of Action*, ed. Richard Kearney (London: Sage Publications, 1996), pp. 81–98.

3. Volume 1 examines the relationship between time and narrative in historical writing. Volume 2 addresses the same theme in relation to fiction and theories of literature. Volume 3 synthesizes and consolidates the ideas developed in volumes 1 and 2. Ricoeur has been consistently concerned with the nature and status of history since his first major work on the topic, *History and Truth,* trans. Charles A. Kelbley (Evanston: Northwestern University Press, 1965), originally published as *Histoire et vérité,* (Paris: Seuil, 1955).

4. White, *The Content of the Form,* p. 171.

5. Ricoeur, "Life in Quest of Narrative," p. 29.

6. Ibid., p. 30.

7. Ricoeur, *TN*1, p. 74.

8. Ricoeur, "On Interpretation" p. 180.

9. This view is associated with both structuralists and non-structuralists alike, such as Frank Kermode, *The Sense of an Ending: Studies in the Theory of Fiction* (Oxford: Oxford University Press, 1967); Seymour Chatman, *Story and Discourse: Narrative Structure in Fiction and Film* (Ithaca and London: Cornell University Press, 1978); and Roland Barthes, *Image, Music, Text* (Fontana Press, 1993), pp. 79–124; as well as historians such as Louis Mink, "Narrative Form as a Cognitive Instrument," pp. 143–44 and Hayden White, "The Value of Narrativity in the Representation of Reality," in *On Narrative,* ed. W. J. T. Mitchell (Chicago: University of Chicago Press, 1981).

10. David Carr, *Time, Narrative and History* (Bloomington, IN: Indiana University Press, 1986), p. 162. However, Carr himself rejects this view of the narrative. His own thesis is closer to Ricoeur's position and claims that narration is not an escape from or distortion of reality; instead of falsifying human life, it extends, enriches, and confirms its primary features such as temporality.

11. Each sense of *mimesis* expresses a relation between

narrative accounts and real life. See chapter 5 of this book for an account of a third delineation of *mimesis* understood as "configuration" or emplotment: a synthesizing activity between individual events and the whole; between heterogeneous elements, agents, goals, interactions, and circumstances; and between episodic and narrative dimensions of time.

12. Ricoeur, *TN*1, p. ix.

13. Ricoeur, *OA*, p. 162.

14. Ricoeur, "Intellectual Autobiography," p. 47.

15. Ricoeur, "Imagination, Testimony and Trust, A dialogue with Paul Ricoeur," p. 15.

16. Ricoeur, *OA*, p. 162.

17. Richard White, *Remembering Ahanagran, Storytelling in a Family's Past* (New York: Hill and Wang, 1998), pp. 271–73.

18. Ibid.

19. Ricoeur, "Narrative Identity," p. 73.

20. Edmund Husserl, *The Phenomenology of Time Consciousness*, trans. James S. Churchill (The Hague: Martinus Nijhoff, 1964).

21. Ricoeur, *TN*1, pp. 252–53.

22. Ricoeur, "The Question of Proof in Freud's Writings," p. 273.

23. Ricoeur, *OA*, p. 114 fn.1.

24. Paul Ricoeur, "Explanation and Understanding: On Some Remarkable Connections Among the Theory of the Text, Theory of Action, and Theory of History," p. 164.

25. Ricoeur, *TN*1, p. 3.

26. Ricoeur, *TN*3, p. 247.

27. Ibid.

28. Freud, "Remembering, Repeating and Working-Through"; Ricoeur, "The Question of Proof in Freud's Writings," p. 253; and Ricoeur, *TN*3, p. 247.

29. In the context of my examination, I pay particular attention to Ricoeur, *Freud and Philosophy: An Essay on Interpretation*, trans. Denis Savage (New Haven: Yale University Press, 1970); Ricoeur, "The Question of Proof in Freud's Writings," pp. 247–73; Ricoeur, "From Psychoanalysis to the Question of the Self, or Thirty Years of Philosophical Work," pp. 68–94; and "Memory and Forgetting," pp. 5–11. I also briefly examine two of Freud's own essays on memory: "Mourning and Melancholia," in *On Metapsychology: The Theory of Psychoanalysis* (London: Penguin, 1984), pp. 251–68 and "Remembering, Repeating and Working-Through."

30. Ricoeur, *Freud and Philosophy*, p. 345.

31. Ibid. Ricoeur specifically addresses critiques of psychoanalysis that emerged out of a symposium held in New York in 1958. Its proceedings were published under the title *Psychoanalysis, Scientific Method and Philosophy*, ed. Sidney Hook (New York: New York University Press, 1959). In particular, Ricoeur draws on three papers from the edited collection: Heinz Hartmann, "Psychoanalysis as a Scientific Theory," pp. 3–37; Ernest Nagel, "Methodological Issues in Psychoanalytic Theory," pp. 38–56; and Michael Scriven, "The Experimental Investigation of Psychoanalysis," pp. 226–51.

32. Ricoeur, *Freud and Philosophy*, p. 346.

33. Ibid.

34. Ibid., p. 364.

35. Ricoeur, "The Question of Proof in Freud's Writings," p. 248.

36. Ibid.

37. Freud, "Remembering, Repeating and Working-Through," p. 154; Ricoeur, "The Question of Proof in Freud's Writings," p. 249.

38. Ibid., p. 251.

39. Ibid.

40. Ibid., p. 253.

41. Ibid.

42. Ricoeur, "Memory and Forgetting," p. 5.

43. Ricoeur, "The Question of Proof in Freud's Writings," p. 254.

44. Freud, "Remembering, Repeating and Working-Through," p. 150.

45. Ibid., p. 151.

46. Ibid., p. 153.

47. Ibid., p. 155.

48. Ricoeur, *TN*3, pp. 246-47. Elsewhere Ricoeur makes the same point in the following way: "[Narrative fiction] is an irreducible dimension of *self-understanding*. If it is true that fiction is only completed in life and that life can be understood only through the stories that we tell about it, then an examined life, in the sense of the word as we have borrowed it from Socrates, is a life *recounted*" ("Life in Quest of Narrative," pp. 30-31).

49. Ricoeur, *OA*, p. 161.

50. Paul Ricoeur, "Autonomie et vulnerabilité," unpublished lecture given at Seance inaugurale du Seminaire de l'IHE (November 6, 1995). Cited in Bernard P. Dauenhauer, *Paul Ricoeur, The Promise and the Risk of Politics* (Lanham, Maryland: Rowman and Littlefield, 1998), p. 124.

51. Ricoeur, "The Question of Proof in Freud's Writings," p. 268.

52. Ricoeur, "Life in Quest of Narrative," p. 30.

Chapter Seven

THE LIMITATIONS OF RICOEUR'S ACCOUNT

Granted Ricoeur's innovative approach to the problem of the self, two objections to his position ought to be considered. The first objection is that Ricoeur is too selective in his choice of both literary genre and psychoanalytic school as sources of narrative form and standards of excellence for accounts of the narrative self. The second is that his treatment of the operations of self-knowledge and self-examination draws him closer to a traditional view of the self he is, supposedly, anxious to eschew.

SELECTIVE APPEALS TO LITERARY AND PSYCHOANALYTIC DISCOURSES

Literature

Ricoeur seems more aware than Dennett of the fact that the choice of narrative genre and the assumption of a particular approach to individual texts make a difference to the interpretation derived on the basis of these commitments. While Dennett, for example, acknowledges that the consideration of thought experiments such as multiple personality or immortality are a means of exploring beliefs and assumptions about selfhood, he seems unaware that the very form of the thought experiment narrative itself is not value neutral. Ricoeur, on the other hand, takes naturalists to task because they choose thought experiments drawn from science over those cases drawn from literature more generally. However, once the way is clear for Ricoeur to appeal to literature for puzzle cases and standards of intelligibility, it could be argued that he assumes the same blinkered vision he attributes to naturalists. This is because he focuses almost exclusively on literary archetypes that tend to support a sense of self as stable and unified rather than fragile.

Ricoeur flags his particular interests through his choice of historical sources (for example, Aristotle's privileging of a tragic hero such as Oedipus—a model of predictability and reliability). Further, with the single exception of Musil's *L'homme Sans Qualités*, he focuses on authors such as Woolf or Proust, whose characters, however unstable, are paragons of steadfastness when compared with the work of other modern writers.[1] I am thinking especially of Samuel Beckett, Harold Pinter, and Thomas Pynchon, who have revolutionized the narrative form and disrupted Aristotelian conventions with an emphasis on discontinuity, disorder, and dissipation. For example, consider Beckett's play, *Not I*, which depicts a

monologue delivered by a disembodied mouth of indeterminate sex.[2] Alternatively, Michael Sprinker draws
attention to Pynchon's novel, *Gravity's Rainbow*, whose
hero, Tyrone Slothrop, originally an ordinary American
soldier, is somehow strewn across Europe after World
War II: "Some believe that fragments of Slothrop have
grown into consistent personae of their own. If so,
there's no telling which of the Zone's present-day popu-
lation are offshoots of his original scattering."[3] In
chapter 5, I argued that Ricoeur opposes the puzzle
cases of literary fiction to the thought experiments of
science in order to peel apart the two senses of identity—*idem* or sameness and *ipse* or selfhood—that he
wants to distinguish. On his account, literary fiction
affords descriptions of characters who, however fragile
they might be, can nevertheless pose the question, "who
am I," in a way that is not wholly exhausted by a list of
characteristics. However, if, as I have suggested, Ricoeur
is selective in his choice of literary paradigms, and if
contemporary literature is far more radical in its questioning of personal identity than traditional genres, then
Ricoeur's strategy of appealing to literary norms fails;
even the question, "who am I," becomes incoherent for
some writers.

Given that literary norms emerge out of particular
historical and cultural contexts, one critic, James Fodor,
argues that Ricoeur's objective to extend the application
of Aristotelian emplotment across narrative traditions is
over-ambitious.[4] In *TN*1, Ricoeur had made the following claim: "The question that I shall continue to
pursue until the end of this work is whether the para-

digm of order, characteristic of tragedy, is capable of extension and transformation to the point where it can be applied to the whole narrative field."[5] First of all, however, there is the question of whether or not Ricoeur has got it right regarding Greek tragedy. Theorists such as Fodor, Hillis Miller, and Pamela Anderson each object to Ricoeur's reading of plays such as *Oedipus Rex* and *Antigone*.[6] Anderson, for example, takes Ricoeur to task for unquestioningly reading *Antigone* through Hegel. Arguing that Ricoeur's Hegelian analysis of Antigone as a woman blindly devoted to traditional family values is mistaken, she challenges his assumption that there can be generic accounts of humanity that endure unchanged.

> So Ricoeur would seem to connect the constancy of mythical narrative with a generic understanding of "the human" and, in particular, the limitations pointed to by the deliberation of the tragic hero or heroine who suffers unjustly but with—apparently blind— steadfastness. . . . However, concerning Antigone's steadfastness, we will read other (female) philosophers [such as Luce Iragaray] who insist over and against Hegel (and so by implication Ricoeur) upon Antigone's tough-minded, not blind devotion to what is both noble and just.[7]

That Ricoeur's reading of Greek tragedy may be challenged by other possible interpretations is not the only difficulty he faces. Fodor in particular challenges Ricoeur's assumption that the account of narrative intelligibility that he derives from Greek tragedy can apply universally. Ricoeur's interest in tragedy is explicitly stated in the following way:

> If the tragedy of *Antigone* can teach us something, it is because the very content of the conflict—despite the lost and unrepeatable character of the mythical ground from which it emerges and of the festive environment surrounding the celebration of the spectacle—has maintained an ineffaceable permanence. The tragedy of *Antigone* touches . . . the agonistic ground of human experience, where we witness the interminable confrontation of man and woman, old age and youth, society and the individual, the living and the dead, humans and gods. Self-recognition is at the price of a difficult apprenticeship acquired over the course of a long voyage through these persistent conflicts, whose universality is inseparable from their particular localization, which is, in every instance, unsurpassable.[8]

Fodor asks what Ricoeur might mean by claiming that the content of tragedy has maintained an "ineffaceable permanence" and argues instead that tragedy cannot be understood separately from its particular, social, political, moral, and religious context: "His account remains parasitic on the practices and content (both moral and religious) of specific narrative traditions."[9] He takes Ricoeur to task, specifically in relation to Aristotle's emphasis on actions he describes as the "feats of outstanding men," which are usually "valiant acts of war," and argues than any given set of virtues is context specific.[10]

> What constitutes fear and pity, let alone what consti-
> tutes virtue and sound ethical judgment, cannot be
> known independent of the particular narrative in
> which those terms are embedded and within which
> they are deployed. Ricoeur, however . . . assumes that
> there is just one universal experience of "the tragic" to
> which all these ethical conflicts point, and that the
> emotions of pity and fear which each of these
> dilemmas cathartically provoke and "purify," carry
> essentially the same cognitive content.[11]

Fodor notes that an early Christian's fear of death (of the
destruction of his or her soul) is not the same as a tragic
hero of ancient Greece's fear (of not dying well). Equally,
the same might be said of the fear of pregnancy or rape
that women from different cultural backgrounds (for
example, Islamic, Hindu, or Christian) might have.

In sum, Ricoeur's appeal to particular literary genres
and their corresponding standards of excellence does
not exhaust the contribution literature makes to philosophical questions about personal identity. Rather, literature taken as a whole is a rich resource for any number
of puzzle cases regarding personal identity, many of
which work to undermine the paradigm of stable selfhood that Ricoeur claims to find there. Moreover, granted
the range of possible interpretations of any given genre
and the variety of literary genres, it seems churlish to
hold one as a standard of excellence for all other narrative traditions.

Psychoanalysis

My concern with psychoanalysis is similar to that raised in chapter 3 regarding Dennett's narrative account of the self. There I argued that Dennett places too great an emphasis on linguistic ability and intellectual capacity as required conditions of selfhood. This objection can also be leveled at Ricoeur because the latter also places an emphasis on narrative capacities and competencies. For example, where Dennett posits narrative richness as a requirement of the fully fledged self, Ricoeur argues for the need to be educated to the level of narrative coherence and identity. Specifically, by appealing to Freudian psychoanalysis, Ricoeur focuses on an approach that designates only that which can be articulated as the proper subject of psychoanalytic investigation. As detailed in chapter 6, the focus of psychoanalytic enquiry is not on observable behavior, but on desire that is expressed in words (for example, reports of dreams or fantasies and the articulation of memories). In choosing Freudian psychoanalysis, Ricoeur ignores several more holistic psychotherapies, such as psychodynamic or gestalt therapies. These are very attuned to the significance of body signals, tone, and posture to the psychoanalytic relationship, as well as to the possibility that repressed memories and emotions may well be best acknowledged, shared, and released through bodily rather than verbal expression.

Although I largely accept the force of this objection, Ricoeur's position can, at the same time, be viewed as a more holistic account of human experience in this regard than Dennett's alternative. Specifically, Ricoeur's emphasis on Freud's original explanation of the operation of memory as "working-through" focuses on memory as a form of *work* and thus recognizes that good stories reflect a manifold of human capabilities that may be investigated in the psychoanalytic situation.[12] Freud's description of working-through as an activity that relates the recounting of experiences with the libidinal forces that invoke or resist their articulation is also consistent with Ricoeur's general thesis that an individual can attest that they persist as a self on the basis of their actions in the world.

Ricoeur's translator, Kathleen Blamey, analyzes the term "work" placing emphasis on its dual nature as a physical as well as intellectual activity. Briefly, it is the activity the analysand undertakes in order to retrieve and rehabilitate unintelligible or unbearable past experiences.

> The term "work" is especially appropriate in the case of psychoanalysis, where it resonates with both a physical and a hermeneutical-productive sense. Work belongs to the physical vocabulary of energy, to the application and displacement of forces. The work of analysis, in this sense, does indeed contend with a complex system of forces and counterforces. . . . Becoming an object of consciousness is best described not through metaphors of the gaze, of contemplation, but through metaphors of exertion, of overcoming obstacles and hidden forces. In fact, until this labor has been performed by the analysand, there can be no progress in converting unconscious to conscious processes and enlarging the sphere of ego in relation to id.[13]

Blamey highlights an important passage in Freud that makes a distinction between "hearing" and "experiencing":

> If we communicate to a patient some idea which he has at one time repressed but which we have discovered in him, our telling him makes at first no change in his mental condition. . . . To have heard something and to have experienced something are in their psychological nature two quite different things.[14]

Invoking the notion of "working-through," as Blamey sees it, means that the process of self-understanding is not a smooth integration of a coherent view. Instead, forces of resistance will disrupt, and repetitions will ensue. Yet perseverance with the analytic work pays off. The ideal outcome of such a process is that there is not just an intellectual refusal or acceptance of an interpretation, but a "conviction based on the lived experience of what is involved in the resistance" and a meaningful and longterm integration of the insight into one's life:

> Working-through allows the subject to move from a purely intellectual refusal or acceptance of an interpretation to a conviction based on the lived experience of what is involved in the resistance. Thus the subject is able not only to recognize the fact of repetitive mechanisms on the intellectual level but becomes capable of realizing this as part of his own experience, not simply of having an insight but of assuming it in a lasting way.[15]

This emphasis Blamey places on the role of "working-through" in the integration of self-interpretations in the life of an individual makes clear and extends what is implicit in Ricoeur's own account of "working-through." It is also underlined in Ricoeur's claim that the presuppositions of the psychoanalyst and analysand encounter are: "(1) desire speaks, (2) it addresses itself to another (parents, the analyst), (3) it enters into a conflict between wanting to know and resistance, (4) it seeks its place in the reconstruction of a narrative identity that is not only understood but accepted."[16] The focus in this passage is not on the idea of self-knowledge based on empirical or cognitive knowledge, but one based on attestation, which, in this case, is the relationship between desire, the self and others, curiosity and fear, understanding and acceptance. This is not a fixed or formulaic list of characteristic features or key events, but a relational "work in progress" that is continuously evolving. What is emphasized here is the corporeal aspect of "working-through" which seeks to narratively articulate the libidinal forces Freud attempted to understand. Ricoeur's notion of narration, then, invokes a concrete and practical engagement with oneself. This distinguishes his account from Dennett's far more abstract and intellectualist notion of narration and draws him closer to the positions of Flanagan and Damasio, summarized in chapter 3, in so far as it incorporates an embodied dimension into the activity of narration. Granted then that Ricoeur's reliance on psychoanalytic standards of excellence is problematic because he appeals to a Freudian psychoanalytic tradition that places emphasis on the articulation and rearticulation of acceptable stories, nevertheless, his position can be expressed in a way that makes it more sensitive to the corporeal character of the psychoanalytic exchange. In this respect at least, Ricoeur's account is more comprehensive than Dennett's, whose emphasis on the linguistic conditions of selfhood, and neglect of the embodied conditions of selfhood, have been demonstrated.

FOCUS ON THE SELF-EXAMINING SELF

The second objection I have to Ricoeur's position is that his account of the narrative self is sometimes more consistent with a traditional view of the self as masterful and authorial than it is with his general posit of the self as provisional, relational, and dynamic. The narrative self, delineated as the "fruit of an examined life," is a concept of the self that Ricoeur himself acknowledges recalls the Socratic ideal.[17] As such, it invokes an implicit judgment about what the "good life" is—the "good life" is the examined life—and can be placed in the same tradition as, for example, the Lockean forensic self, whose conscience accuses or excuses her on the Last Day.[18] Indeed, Ricoeur argues that narrative coherence is a prerequisite of autonomy:

> In this respect, one can speak of education to narrative coherence, of education to narrative identity. One can learn to tell the same story otherwise, learn to let it be told by others than oneself, learn to submit the

narrative of one's life to the critique of documentary
history. These are practices that can take charge, on
the narrative level, of the paradox of autonomy and
fragility. We therefore say that to be autonomous one
must be a subject capable of leading one's life in
accord with the idea of narrative coherence.[19]

What is clear from this passage is that Ricoeur has a particular task for the concept of the self to do—to act as a
source of moral capacities—in this case, autonomy.
There is, of course, nothing implicitly wrong with this
strategy; it is neither incoherent nor implausible. However, it is inconsistent with his earlier claim, outlined in
chapter 4, that the capable self, of which the narrative
self is a manifestation, captures the boundary conditions
of human existence. The "educated" narrative self as one
moment of the capable self is a normative ideal, not a
shared condition. This is because not all human lives
follow a trajectory of the kind that Ricoeur has in mind.
Margaret Walker makes this point in her objection to the
narrative theories of Bernard Williams and Charles Taylor,
but it can equally be applied to Ricoeur:

There is just no plausible move in general from
making sense of an action in some narrative context to
needing to see it against the backcloth of an entire life.
It is also because I find the more ambitious claims
about the inclusiveness and centrality of plans, projects, and plots questionable as descriptions of actual
people's actual lives, where these lives nonetheless
seem decent, good, or admirable.[20]

The point is that many (or most?) people's lives are far too fragmented and piece-meal to be easily emplotted or appropriated into the themes, projects, or unities that are required for the purposes of "self-examination," or at least for the level of self-examination that Ricoeur seems to demand.

Essentially, my objection to Ricoeur's position is that his delineation of "self-examination" as a mode of "self-knowledge" makes the assumption that the aims and methods of these operations are uncontested and transparent. Michel Foucault has strongly challenged any such complacency with regard to the operations of self-knowledge. In his later writings on the self, Foucault highlights the numerous ways in which the task of self-knowledge has been carried out in different historical periods.[21] Foucault describes these different operations of self-knowledge as "technologies of the self" which "permit individuals to effect by their own means or with the help of others a certain number of operations on their own bodies and souls, thoughts, conduct, and way of being, so as to transform themselves in order to attain a certain state of happiness, purity, wisdom, perfection, or immortality."[22] Briefly, Foucault is sensitive to the personal, moral, and political implications of privileging one mode of self-knowledge over another. As an example, he compares Stoic Greco-Roman practices (in the first two centuries AD) with Christian monastic principles developed in the late Roman Empire (fourth and fifth centuries). According to Foucault, the aim of self-knowledge for the Stoics (inspired by Seneca 2 BC–65 AD and Marcus Aurelius 121–80 AD) was mastery of the body as well as the soul. In turn, self-examination involved the administrative task of taking stock of deeds done and undone as well as meditative practices and physical training.[23] Alternatively, for Foucault, the aim of self-knowledge in early Christianity was the renunciation of the self, not its mastery. In turn, the paradigm of self-examination was the confessional where attention focused on the seeking out and verbalizing of bad intentions and faults, and on the doer or sinner rather than the deed or sin. This verbalization is described by Foucault as the precursor to Freudian psychoanalysis. It is the "touchstone or the money of thought," implying that there is something hidden, or permanently elusive in us, which once disclosed must be renounced.[24]

If we accept Foucault's claim that the practices of self-examination are not neutral techniques, and that any given interrogation of the self will find only the reflection its modes and methods are fitted to recognize, Ricoeur's selective treatment of literary genres and psychoanalytic schools makes more sense. His account of narrative self-examination may be viewed as being fuelled by his ambition to deliver a particular kind of self—one capable of a particular kind of moral agency. It is this ambition that leads him to focus on those aspects of literature and psychoanalysis that lend support to his claims that the self can be stabilized through narrative coherence, and that one should ignore those aspects of either discourse that undermine that very stability.

However, granted the diversity of narrative forms and formlessness, narrative unity is not something Ricoeur can take for granted. Gary Greenberg captures the way in which narrative language invokes a kind of circularity in the following terms:

> In the play we have been thrust into, narrative is cast as a "capacity" or a "tool," which of course is the possession of the single authorial entity. But behind the scenes, before such a formulation can make sense, an agreement must already have been struck that we are unitary beings with psychological essences. The pervasiveness of the essentialist drama is such that it forecloses other possibilities, for instance the possibility that the narrative grips us, that we are a capacity or tool of narrative. . . .Once cast as unitary selves, it is almost impossible to see that there are other stories about what selves are.[25]

For Greenberg, the language of narrative seduces us into an essentialist drama where we see ourselves as the central protagonists forging a destiny that preserves our unity and integrity. The price of such unity is the exclusion of the "otherness" of narrative: the fact that it is narrative that constitutes us as self-constituting beings.

> To conceive the self as author may be to give an adequate description of a kind of human selfhood, but this is just one among many possible stories about what a self is. It is a seductive story, offering us the authorial power that we capture in terms like "responsibility for oneself" or "shaping one's destiny" or "capacity for storytelling"—terms that preserve the unitary subject's place at the center of his or her narrative world. But we are seduced at a price: the erasure

of the fundamental otherness of narrative, its exceeding and constituting us, albeit as beings who constitute ourselves.[26]

In this passage, Greenberg reflects a postmodern dis-ease with the language of narrative unity. This is the dis-ease of postmodern philosophers such as Foucault, Jacques Derrida, Julia Kristeva, and Judith Butler, who question both traditional notions of the self as a single persisting unity and the authority and mastery of the liberal ideal of autonomous agency associated with it. Roughly speaking, the postmodern alternative is the notion of the self as an unstable locus of social and historical influences—an indeterminate, fragmented willow-the-wisp: "I myself, at the deepest level of my wants and desires, am unsure, centerless, and divided."[27] If Ricoeur, for example, asks, "For the question of the capable person is, successively, the question of determining who can speak, who can act, who can recount, who can impute actions to himself or herself?" Foucault problematizes such a line of questioning.[28]

We would no longer hear the questions that have been rehashed for so long: Who really spoke? Is it really he and not someone else? With what authenticity or originality? And what part of his deepest self did he express in his discourse? Instead there would be other questions, like these: What are the modes of existence of this discourse? Where has it been used, how can it circulate, and who can appropriate it for himself? What are the places in it where there is room for possible subjects? Who can assume these various subject functions? And behind all these questions, we would hear hardly anything but the stirring of an indifference: What difference does it make who is speaking?[29]

For Foucault, there are not subjects or selves so much as there are subject positions within discursive practices, which may or may not be available to an individual at any given historical moment.

If we were to accept the objections of thinkers such as Greenberg and Foucault to the seductive form of the narrative, we would have to conclude that Ricoeur's warrant for attributing a narrative unity to the self, based on particular standards of coherence and intelligibility, is not justified. It turns out that any given account of the narrative self, whether drawn from literature or psychoanalysis, is far more fragile than Ricoeur wants to allow. His position seems, inevitably, to slide closer to postmodern accounts of subjectivity, and to Dennett's naturalist account of the fictional self whose "only momentum," in Dennett's terms, "is the stability imparted to it by the web of beliefs that constitute it."[30]

The question then arises—how much further have we moved from the traditional antinomy that our usual sense of self as a unity of thoughts, experiences, and actions must either refer to something substantial or be illusory? If we follow the familiar Cartesian path we are lead to a rational, self-contained model of subjectivity. If we follow Dennett's path, we must conclude that our usual sense of self is indeed mistaken and founded, at best, on a theoretical abstraction. Similarly, if we follow Greenberg et al., we seem to be left with disintegration and fragmentation. Alternatively, however, if we travel

Ricoeur's phenomenological trail, which acknowledges the boundary conditions constraining our interpretation of the world and of ourselves, we must conclude that the antinomy is a false one; it is not a choice between substance and illusion. One critic, Morny Joy, who also privileges Ricoeur's account of the narrative self over others, makes a similar point: It is not a simple choice between rational control and self-containment and pathological dysfunction.

> The enlightened Western tradition and much of psychoanalysis, however, continues to project an image of mastery, of rational self-containment. When it is challenged, it often seems to imply that the only alternative is a type of pathological disintegration where all control and standards are abandoned. . . . Neither takes into account the constant interplay of an embodied and emotional subject in a life-world where constellations of identity are formed and reformed. Identity is not something bestowed or definitively attained. Nor is it infinitely inaccessible or irrevocable.[31]

In brief, it is the embodied and temporal nature of the narrative self that prevents it from solidifying into substance on the one hand, or dissipating into ether on the other. For example, if we accept that corporeality is basic to the human condition, then the possibility of a human being having a disembodied substantial self is incoherent. On the other hand, the very nature of human embodiment means that different dimensions of human identity (for example, being female or visually impaired) cannot be instantly transformed by a simple act of will—

corporeality lends a stability to the narrative self. Further, if we accept Ricoeur's account of the temporal nature of human actions and practices, we need not view selfhood as a momentary flash that quickly fades, but as a unity that endures for short or long periods of time.

Ricoeur's later work, which revisits his narrative project as a whole, adds a further dimension to his consideration of time. It addresses both the task of history and the notion of "memory as work" from the perspective of a historian of justice. For Ricoeur, any account of narrative identity—individual or collective—must acknowledge a debt to the past. This claim was initially posited in *TN*1: "[W]e tell stories because in the last analysis human lives need and merit being narrated. This remark takes on its full force when we refer to the necessity to save the history of the defeated and the lost. The whole history of suffering cries out for vengeance and calls for narrative."[32] However, a debt to the past was not the focus of the subsequent volumes of *TN*, nor of *OA*. In his later writing, however, Ricoeur attempts to redress this imbalance. He admits that while the idea of the capable self was developed in *OA*, those forces which prevent individuals from acting and contribute to their suffering were not sufficiently acknowledged with regard to each of the four levels of action: [1] speaking, [2] acting, [3] narrating, and [4] imputing.

[1] However, I did not emphasize enough our difficulty, even our incapacity to bring to language the emotional, often traumatic experience that psychoanalysis attempts to liberate. . . .

[2] I left unclear the face of impotence that goes with this ability [to speak], owing not only to those infir-

mities of every sort that may affect the human body as the organ of action, but also to the interference of outside powers capable of diminishing, hindering, or preventing our use of our abilities.

[3] [T]he employment of this capacity [to narrate] does not always happen smoothly, as is indicated by the inability of many survivors of extermination camps to bring their wounded memories to verbal expression in narrative. . . .

[4] These incapacities [to be accountable], which affect the imputability of human action, today pose serious problems for educators, judges, and political leaders inasmuch as they diminish what we can call our aptitude for citizenship.[33]

The history then of the suffering subject as much as the acting subject must, for Ricoeur, be a feature of any acceptable narrative; it is the therapeutic function of narrative that can heal a "wounded memory." In this way, the silenced voices and neglected pain of marginalized individuals and groups can be retrieved and refigured as part of personal and collective identities.

History is not limited to describing and explaining past facts—or let us say, what actually happened—it can also take the risk of resuscitating and reanimating the unkept promises of the past. In this way, it rejoins what people who have disappeared may have imagined and frees it from the contingency of unachieved realizations so as to hand it over to the imagination of the future.[34]

On an individual level, Ricoeur's challenge can be understood to imply that any narrative account of a human life must view the identity of the self in relational terms, in particular in terms of the forces of oppression and exclusion that operate discursively, practically, and politically. On a collective level, it implies that the narrative identity of any group, such as those based on sex or ethnic origin, must pay attention to the ways in which different voices have been silenced or excluded in order that different identities are established.

This account of what is proper to narrative identity is one that is far more engaged with the concrete and inter-subjective lives of human beings than it is to the idealized model of self-contained autonomy that Ricoeur's account of self-examination initially prompted. In addition, it draws Ricoeur's graft of phenomenology and hermeneutics further away from the modernist notion that knowledge can be value neutral. Specifically, his account of narrative as a tool of justice is consistent with Foucault's thesis that knowledge is a practice of power.[35] For Foucault, "power is everywhere; not because it embraces everything, but because it comes from everywhere ... power is not an institution, and not a structure; neither is it a certain strength we are endowed with; it is the name that one attributes to a complex strategical situation in a particular society."[36] It could be argued that Ricoeur's expanded understanding of narrative intelligibility captures the nuanced way in which power operates in the constitution of personal and collective identities and thereby reflects a similar sensitivity to the operations of power to that of Foucault.

NOTES TO CHAPTER 7

1. Robert Musil, *L'homme sans qualities* (Paris: Seuil, 1979). Another exception might be Virginia Woolf's *Orlando*, (Oxford: Oxford University Press, 1998), whose protagonist lives through several centuries, exchanging gender, occupation, and lovers along the way. Ricoeur focuses on the trials of Mrs. Dalloway and, to my knowledge, makes no mention of the adventures of Orlando.

2. Samuel Beckett, *Not I*, in *Collected Shorter Plays: Samuel Beckett* (New York: Grove Press, 1984).

3. From Thomas Pynchon's *Gravity's Rainbow*, cited in Michael Sprinker, "Fictions of the Self: The End of Autobiography," in *Autobiography: Essays Theoretical and Critical*, ed. James Olney (Princeton: Princeton University Press, 1980), p. 321.

4. James Fodor, "The Tragic Face of Narrative Judgment: Christian Reflections on Paul Ricoeur's Theory of Narrative," in *Paul Ricoeur and Narrative*, ed. Morny Joy (Alberta: University of Calgary Press, 1997).

5. Ricoeur, *TN*1, p. 38.

6. Miller, *Reading Narrative*; Pamela Anderson, "Re-reading Myth in Philosophy: Hegel, Ricoeur and Irigaray Reading Antigone," in *Paul Ricoeur and Narrative*, pp. 51–68.

7. Anderson, "Re-reading Myth in Philosophy," p. 52.

8. Ricoeur, *OA*, p. 243.

9. Fodor, "The Tragic Face of Narrative Judgment," p. 154.

10. Ibid., p. 158.

11. Ibid., p. 161.

12. Susan Brison offers some new insights into the operation of memory which further underline its complexity when she discusses the way in which people who have undergone traumatic events, such as survivors of rape or veterans of war,

"remember" their past horrors both cognitively and psychosomatically (Susan J. Brison, "Outliving Oneself: Trauma, Memory, and Personal Identity," in *Feminists Rethink the Self*, ed. Diana Tietzens Meyers [Boulder, CO: Westview Press, 1997], pp. 12–39).

13. Kathleen Blamey, "From the Ego to the Self: A Philosophical Itinerary," in *The Philosophy of Paul Ricoeur*, ed. Lewis Edwin Hahn (Chicago and La Salle, IL: Open Court, 1995), p. 595.

14. Sigmund Freud, "The Unconscious," in *Standard Edition of the Complete Psychological Works of Sigmund Freud* 14, ed. James Strachey in collaboration with Anna Freud (London: Hogarth Press, 1964), p. 168. Cited in Blamey, "From the Ego to the Self: A Philosophical Itinerary," p. 595.

15. Ibid., p. 599.

16. Ricoeur in Thelma Lavine, "Ricoeur and the Conflict of Interpretations," in *The Philosophy of Paul Ricoeur*, pp. 191–92.

17. Ricoeur, *TN*3, pp. 246–47.

18. Locke's conceptualization of the self was largely driven by his ambition to deliver a morally responsible and accountable entity: "But in the great Day, wherein the Secrets of all Hearts shall be laid open, it may be reasonable to think, no one shall be made to answer for what he knows nothing of; but shall receive his Doom, his Conscience accusing or excusing him" (John Locke, *An Essay Concerning Human Understanding* II, pp. xxvii, 22) In this passage, Locke posits "conscience" (a 17th-century synonym for consciousness) as the ground of blame and praise.

19. Paul Ricoeur, "Autonomie et vulnerabilité," p. 124.

20. Margaret Urban Walker, *Moral Understandings* (London: Routledge, 1998), p. 148.

21. Foucault claims that one of the main principles of personal and social conduct in early Greek philosophy was the

precept "to take care of yourself," and that the notion of self-knowledge, famously articulated by the Delphic oracle, appeared only as a consequence of taking this care. Foucault himself borrows the earlier term in order to underline his claim that the way in which the self is interrogated has profound implications for ethical theory and practice (Michel Foucault, *The Care of the Self: The History of Sexuality* 3, trans. Robert Hurley [London: Penguin, 1986]).

22. Michel Foucault, "Technologies of the Self," p. 18.

23. Ibid., pp. 19-43. Meditation (melete) involves imagining worst possible scenarios in order to cultivate acceptance while bodily self-control (gymnasia) involves abstinence in order to test the independence of individuals vis-à-vis the external world.

24. Ibid., p. 47.

25. Gary Greenberg, "If a self is a Narrative: Social Constructionism in the Clinic," *Journal of Narrative and Life History* 5, no. 3 (1995): 273.

26. Ibid., pp. 272-73.

27. Julia Kristeva, *In the Beginning was Love: Psychoanalysis and Faith*, trans. A. Goldhammer (New York: Columbia University Press, 1987), p. 8. I grant that this is, indeed, a very rough definition of postmodern subjectivity. In particular, I suggest that this applies, in the main, only to the early writings of the authors mentioned. Each of them in their later works has modified their positions to a large degree.

28. Ricoeur, "From Psychoanalysis to the Question of the Self, or Thirty Years of Philosophical Work," p. 89.

29. Michel Foucault, "What is an Author?" in *Essential Works of Foucault* 2, 1954-1984, ed. James D. Faubion (New York: The New Press, 1994), p. 222.

30. Dennett, *CE*, p. 423.

31. Morny Joy, "Writing as Repossession: The Narratives of Incest Victims," in *Paul Ricoeur and Narrative*, p. 46.

32. Ricoeur, *TN* 1, p. 75.

33. Ricoeur, "A Response by Paul Ricoeur," trans. David Pellauer, in *Paul Ricoeur and Narrative*, pp. xl. See also Ricoeur, *The Just*.

34. Ibid., p. xliv.

35. Michel Foucault, *Discipline and Punish*, trans. A. M. Sheridan-Smith (London: Smith, Allen Lane, 1977); *The History of Sexuality* 1, trans. Robert Hurley (London: Penguin, 1978); "The Subject and Power," in *Michel Foucault: Beyond Structuralism and Hermeneutics*, ed. Hubert L. Dreyfus and Paul Rabinow (Chicago: University of Chicago Press, 1982).

36. Foucault, *The History of Sexuality* 1, p. 93.

Conclusion

ASSESSMENT

In the introduction to this text I set myself the task of assessing the merits of two competing narrative theories of the self—one drawn from the analytic tradition, the other from continental philosophy. In subsequent chapters, I examined these theories in terms of their ontological oomph—how they understood the status of the narrative self as real or fictional—and in terms of their epistemological oomph—the degree to which they were able to distinguish between true and false narrative selves. While the results have been mixed—both theories exhibit varied strengths and weaknesses—I conclude that what makes Ricoeur's theory of the self more comprehensive than Dennett's alternative is his rejection of the ontological givens of the objectivist stance and his richer and more philosophically fundamental account of the human world. What emerges is an account of the narrative self that acknowledges the boundary conditions of human existence and captures some key elements of human experience.

THE ONTOLOGICAL STATUS OF THE NARRATIVE SELF

Chapters 1 and 2 examined Dennett's particular naturalist—mild realist—approach to the self, which aims to be objectivist but not reductionist. On the one hand, he seeks to disengage the language of the self from bogus dualisms. On the other, he seeks to prevent its dissipation and replacement by the language of the neurosciences. Drawing on the insights of neuroscience, cognitive psychology, and computational theory, his negative thesis is his rejection of Cartesian influenced views of the self as a persisting substance based on a view of consciousness as a stream-like unity. His positive thesis is that the self is a fiction because, based on a view of consciousness understood in the computational terms of the Multiple Draft Model (MDM), it is unstable and fragmented. Drawing on the insights of evolutionary theory, he further argues that the self is a fiction because human beings are disposed to distinguish themselves from others by telling stories about themselves. Appealing to his heterophenomenological method (HM), he concludes that the self as fictional is not fantastical, and he posits it as a theoretical abstraction and a center of narrative gravity because, for him, while it is not real in the way that brain processes and structures are real, it still has a role in explaining and predicting human behavior. The resulting conceptualization of the self comprises of the integration of narratives about events in a human life. These narratives are spun in a social context and lead any given reader or interpreter to treat the individual to whom they refer *as if* they are (for the most part) a single continuous self.

In the conclusion of chapter 3, however, I argued that Dennett's privileging of objectivist scientific methodologies entails that the world he is interested in is a world that is ultimately populated by scientifically determinable and measurable entities, abstractions, processes, and actions. In sum, his commitment to mild realism and the HM is problematic. While the HM is cast as a method that takes first-person reports of experience seriously, its terms of reference are inconsistent, and it ultimately trumps scientifically determinable phenomena (brains and bodies) over psychological phenomena (first-person accounts of experience). Ultimately, the narrative self is cast as referring to neurophysiological processes that are so dissonant as to offer little support to our usual sense of self. Moreover, even where the HM advises that we take a third-person stance toward the first-person narratives of human beings, it yields an impoverished concept of the self, useful only because of its predictive power. Finally, I argued that Dennett's commitment to the objectivist stance, which forces him to replace one objectivist view of the self (as a substance) with another (as a fiction), is unquestioned and philosophically suspect. If we take Husserl's phenomenological step back (which privileges the description of direct experience over other discourses, including scientific discourses) seriously, then Dennett's privileging of a naturalist stance requires justification.

Where Dennett privileges scientific perspectives and methodologies over first-person accounts of experience,

Ricoeur radically distinguishes between psychological and neuroscientific approaches and language. His strategy, summarized in chapter 4, is to graft the phenomenological step back with the hermeneutic detour through interpretation. This leads him to posit conditions that are prior to the intelligibility of the naturalist objectivist stance. First, he claims that the reflexive, corporeal, intentional, temporal, and intersubjective features of human existence are the conditions of the possibility of putting questions about anything at all, including questions about consciousness and the self. Second, he claims that any given account of human existence is mediated through culturally available discourses, no one of which is privileged a priori. In sum, Ricoeur's thesis is that the self is best understood as a culturally mediated unity that is constrained by the boundary conditions of human existence.

So, like Dennett, Ricoeur can argue that an account of the self as substantial is problematic because the concept of the self does not have an ontological referent—it is not a thing, substance, organization, or further fact. But, unlike Dennett, Ricoeur can avoid the conclusion that the self must be, as a consequence, fictional or irrelevant. He argues instead that the boundary conditions of human existence such as temporality and embodiment give support to a sense of self that is prior to either dualist or reductionist explanations. He posits the notion of the capable self, defined as a unity of action, to express the various ways in which human activities—speaking, acting, narrating, and imputing—are unified, sometimes strongly, sometimes weakly. Specifically, Ricoeur posits narrative recounting—which involves treating the actions and events of a human life as a text to be interpreted—as a successful means of unifying the self over time.

THE EPISTEMOLOGICAL STATUS OF THE NARRATIVE SELF

While Dennett seems happy to admit that his account of the narrative self is epistemologically fragile, Ricoeur's challenge to traditional epistemologies—that the self is not the kind of entity that can be measured in terms of rationalist and empiricist truth conditions—strikes me as an important insight. For Ricoeur, what is epistemologically interesting about the self is in dispute, and his accounts of *ipse*-identity and attestation provide alternative approaches to the problem of identity and self-knowledge to those of traditional methodologies (including Dennett's).

For example, both Dennett and Ricoeur argue that Cartesian solutions to the problem of personal identity that appeal to the continuity of consciousness are doomed to fail. However, what makes Ricoeur's account more adequate and more comprehensive than Dennett's is that Ricoeur also argues an alternative ground of selfhood is possible, and an alternative source of temporal unity can be determined—the capable self narratively identified. Where Dennett, for example, views the discontinuity of consciousness and the fragmentation of memory as evidence that we cannot determine the identity of the self over time (chapter 3), Ricoeur takes the same discontinuity as evidence that the process of becoming a self is a dynamic and creative one. In Ricoeur's case, the focus is on memory, not as an internal and unstable activity, but as work—an ongoing intersubjective struggle to resist incoherence and overcome lapses in order to create meaning (chapter 6).

Again, both Dennett and Ricoeur acknowledge that accounts of the self cannot be assessed by standard empirical test and experiment. However, while Dennett takes this as an argument in favor of reducing the self to a wholly fictional status that ultimately appeals to scientifically determinable criteria in order to distinguish between true and false accounts of selfhood, Ricoeur attests accounts of the self against literary and psychoanalytic standards. It has to be acknowledged, however, that Ricoeur's account of narrative intelligibility is not without its own difficulties. As I argued in chapter 7, whatever the advantages of Ricoeur's general account of attestation, his claims regarding narrative attestation are too strong because narratives take different forms and only some of these provide the kind of stability that Ricoeur would be happy with, namely the idealization of a particular type of human life. Moreover, the model of intersubjective, articulated self-examination, which Ricoeur draws from Freudian psychoanalysis and which forms the basis of his understanding of autonomous action, is only one such model, but there are others. In effect, his account of the narrative self as the fruit of an examined life is a normative ideal, not a shared condition.

In sum, I agree with Ricoeur that narrative attestation permits us to measure accounts of selfhood in terms other than rationalist or empirical standards of truth. Further, I agree that these standards are historically and culturally embedded. Where I disagree, however, is in the implication that such embeddedness has for any given accounts of the self. Where Ricoeur assumes that the narrative form takes a particular kind of shape and appeals to particular sets of competencies, I would argue that the narrative form is far more context sensitive. It follows that the meaning—even the possibility—of the question, "Who am I?" at any given time and for any given narrator and/or audience is, inevitably, far more tentative than even Ricoeur would allow. Even so, I have also argued that there are limits on the kind of self that it is possible to get. In short, there are boundary conditions to the self, such as embodiment and temporality, which ensure that however provisional our identity is at any given time, it is no willow-the-wisp. Furthermore, following the later writings of Ricoeur and Foucault, there is a requirement that narrative accounts view the self as being constituted, in part, in relation to other selves and practices of power.

A brief sketch of the narrative self that emerges provides a plausible antidote to Descartes' excessive rationalism, Dennett's excessive objectivism, and the excessive deconstructionism of post-modernity. It is neither substance nor illusion, but a culturally mediated narrative unity that captures what it is about an individual's life that matters most to her. It is what an individual sees as constituting her and it is consistent with what she actually does. Moreover, not any tall tale will do; the best story that answers the question, "Who am I?" at any given time, or over time, is one that is attested in terms of the following:

- *standards of intersubjective acceptability*—it is credible to the individual and to others;
- *actual historical events*—it is consistent with what happened;
- *emotional depth*—it is emotionally intelligible to the individual themselves and to others;
- *identification*—it captures features that are meaningful to the individual;
- *contextualization*—it is critically examined through the lens of culturally available forms of selfhood; and
- *justice*—it is constituted with an awareness that personal and group identities are forged within relations of power which permit, silence and subdue different forms of human selfhood.

THE PRACTICAL SELF

The diverse approaches to conceptualizing the self that have been explored in these chapters prompt an important question. What is it that we want the notion of self to do? Traditional accounts of personal identity are riddled with problems because theorists have assumed too much about the ontological and epistemological categories within which they worked and said too little about the tasks they hoped their accounts of the self to achieve. In these theories, questions about the constitution of the self have been driven by moral concerns about the kind of beings humans aspire to be, and these two ways of understanding human beings—ontologically and morally—have been posited as importantly related.[1] For example, it is arguable that the 17th-century account of the self posited by John Locke, viewed as one of the first philosophers to take the problem of personal identity seriously, was constrained by Locke's aim to account for such things as personal immortality, self-concern, and moral accountability. Confronted in his world by war, widespread disease, economic and social upheaval, and in his reflections by medical and technological discoveries, the mysteries of Christian faith and immortality, it could be argued that Locke favored a conception of the self as something like a substance, an "all or nothing" unchanging core to give continuity and meaning to human life.

The sense of the self as a moral agent—an originator of actions accountable for them—seems, in the Judaeo-Christian West at least, to be an almost indispensable notion in everyday human exchanges as well as in legal and political life. The continuity and texture of all kinds of relationships with children, friends, and lovers or bankers, builders, and bakers seem to depend on a range of moral notions—promise-keeping, sincerity, fidelity, honesty, integrity, and, when things go wrong, accountability. Equally, the smooth functioning of civil and public life seems to require that crimes are punishable and politicians are held responsible. A concept of self that invokes this kind of accountability might, on these grounds, be posited as an almost primitive or a priori notion that is, somehow, an essential and universal feature of human existence. Certainly, Ricoeur's account of self-examination as a requirement of moral autonomy indicates that he believes this to be the case.

However, just as difficulties can be raised regarding the constitution of the self, so also questions may be raised regarding the stability and transparency of the cluster of moral concepts associated with it. In contrast to the Lockean world, Western society of the 21st century is confronted with racial, ethnic, gender, class and social polarities, the possibility of global warfare, and the probability of global environmental disasters. Furthermore, medical and scientific advances have enabled different kinds of investigations into the human brain, raising new questions about its composition, functions, and capacity while a communications revolution has occurred that greatly surpasses the invention of print in its implications for social change. In addition, institutions such as religion and the heterosexual family, as well as the monolithic, monocultural belief systems that supposedly held reality firm, or at least delivered the ideology of stability, have been radically challenged. In the face of such radical social and technological transformations, the theoretical and moral questions of the 21st century, where humanity is increasingly described as fragmented, alienated, and unstable, are very different from those of the 17th century.

Granted the contextual nature of our questions, the idea that any successful theory of the self must deliver

moral agency in the traditional Lockean sense of the self
as a rational accountable being assumes that the Lockean
view of what moral agency involves is unproblematic. I
reject this assumption because I believe, along with post-
modernists such as Foucault and ethical theorists such as
Walker, that the moral realm is inhabited more by concrete, localized, and intersubjective relations than it is by
autonomous, rational choosers. My point is that the
failure of a theory of the self to deliver moral agency in
the accepted sense does not make a prima facie case for
rejecting it. Rather, what it implies is that traditional
notions of selfhood and moral agency may need to be re-
evaluated and notions of responsibility and punishment
revised or rejected.

One ethical arena where traditional assumptions
about selfhood and moral agency have been challenged
in recent years is healthcare. Since the early eighties, an
increasing number of ethicists working in healthcare
have begun to turn their attention to alternative
approaches to describing and understanding the various
elements of moral life. One such approach deploys narrative concepts and methodologies drawn from philosophers such as Ricoeur and MacIntyre as tools of moral
understanding and assessment. In common with contemporary thinkers in other disciplines who have turned
their attention to narratives, ethicists in the healthcare
arena argue that the first-person narrative, or personal
story, is a rich medium for qualitative data about the
unique lives of individual people. Further, for some of
these theorists, the narrative is not only an important
form of communication, it is also a means of making

human life, and specifically the moral life, intelligible.[2] While they deploy narrative tools in different ways, I suggest that all of these thinkers are engaged in "narrative ethics."[3]

Martha Nussbaum, for example, views literature as a vast resource of moral knowledge and a means of sensitizing people to the responsibilities, obligations, and challenges of a full moral life.[4] Alternatively, the narrative approaches of Albert Jonsen, Stephen Toulmin, and John Arras take a casuistic turn and resolve ethical dilemmas in health care by comparing each new situation with others and with paradigm cases.[5] These authors argue that local, contingent moral rules and maxims to guide action can be derived from paying attention to the morally relevant similarities and differences between cases.

Taking a particularly Ricoeurian approach, Rita Charon suggests that the understanding of a clinical case will be greatly enhanced if attention is paid to its narrative elements (for example, how the case is narrated and who narrates it, the way in which the plot or case develops, and the way in which participants and/or reader(s) respond to and interpret it).[6] In addition to supporting Charon's view, Tod Chambers has sparked a lively debate in the bioethics community with the argument that the task of reporting cases is, itself, not a neutral enterprise.[7] This is because, he argues, the process of describing any set of events involves decisions about including or excluding certain pieces of information and making choices about the way different facts are presented. In this, Chambers is consistent with Ricoeur's hermeneutic position discussed in chapter 7, which acknowledges that the choice of thought experiment or puzzle-case to illustrate certain features of the world contributes to the way in which those features are understood.

Finally, ethicists such as Howard Brody, Arthur Frank, Alasdair MacIntyre, Kathryn Montgomery Hunter, and Hilde Lindemann Nelson argue that the narrative approach to morally difficult situations not only enhances existing models of decision making such as deontological, utilitarian, or principlist approaches, but that the narrative approach is, itself, theoretically robust and provides an alternative means of justifying ethical decisions which focus on the relational and communicative dimensions of moral situations.[8]

Because narrative ethics is in its early stages of development, there is, as yet, no ready-to-hand canonical position that best expresses its central tenets. Indeed, as I have indicated, narrative ethics comprises of a very diverse range of thinkers ranging from those who view narratives as a rich resource for existing ethical theories, to those who see the concepts and methodologies associated with the study of narratives as the foundation of a bioethical theory that can serve as an alternative to traditional approaches. Even so, in what follows, I will combine the account of the Ricoeurian narrative self that I have drawn in earlier chapters with the narrative understandings of theorists, such as Brody and Nelson, to sketch what I see as the most plausible and defensible account of the central tenets of narrative ethics, as it applies to ethical decision making in the healthcare arena:[9]

1. On the narrative view, every moral situation is unique and unrepeatable, and its meaning cannot be fully captured by appealing to universal norms or principles. Understanding an individual's life as a story and deploying narrative methodologies to read and interpret it broadens and enriches our understanding of that life and deepens our insight into the relationship between the unraveling of an individual life and moral agency. Brody argues: "The concept of 'story' suggests appreciation of a narrative mode—that certain sorts of events can be fully understood only as portions of certain ongoing narratives and not as disconnected events occurring in isolation."[10] For Brody, any given clinical decision or ethical choice should not be uncoupled from the whole person and evaluated solely in terms of clinical norms or ethical principles. Rather, decisions should be made in the context of an individual's whole life story.

2. The first person narrative is privileged. In health care settings, this means that the patient's own account, where it is possible to hear it—of his illness, his preferences, his needs—is considered profoundly important. However, as indicated above in relation to the narrative self, personal accounts can be interpreted and attested against various standards including intersubjective acceptability, contextualization, and justice. This means that any individual's testimony must be considered in light of the stories of others and in acknowledgement of the socio-cultural context

within which any narrative is allowed to be told, heard, and understood.

This idea of testing personal narratives against various criteria is somewhat similar to the way in which the principlist model of decision making tries to reduce conflict among beliefs by fitting them into a coherent whole. In the case of principlism, four principles—autonomy, nonmaleficence, beneficence, and justice—are prima facie privileged, and may be modified subsequently through what Beauchamp and Childress call a process of reflective equilibrium.[11] On the narrative view, it is first-person narratives that are prima facie privileged; however, like principles, they can be challenged and modified in the process of what I call a narrative reflective equilibrium, or what Ricoeur might call an "examined life."[12]

A narrative approach of this kind has recently contributed to discussion and debate in relation to end of life decisions. For example, it informs one of the recommendations of the US Council on Ethical and Judicial Affairs, which suggests that when it comes to making decisions for incompetent patients, one of the tasks of a surrogate decision-maker is to consider "how the patient constructed his or her identity or life story" in order to reach a decision about a proposed course of treatment that continues the story "in a manner that is meaningful and consistent with the patient's self-conception."[13] In addition, the Council argues that it is precisely the fact that a number of different options might be consistent with a person's life story which makes the narrative approach so attractive, because it avoids having to predict only a single course of action as compatible and, therefore, morally acceptable.[14]

3. The third tenet of narrative ethics is the claim that the task of moral justification is not primarily a unifying one. Where, for example, principlism takes a systematic approach to ethical decision-making and aims through reflective equilibrium to render our deeply and confidently held moral convictions into a consistent and unified approach, narrative ethics acknowledges and embraces the multiplicity of often contested meanings that are available in any given situation. The task of narrative equilibrium is not to reduce competing perspectives to a commonly shared view, but more to involve as many people as possible in the dialogue. Anne Hudson Jones summarizes this view:

> In ideal form, narrative ethics recognizes the primacy of the patient's story but encourages multiple voices to be heard and multiple stories to be brought forth by all those whose lives will be involved in the resolution of a case. Patient, physician, family, health professional, friend, and social worker, for example, may all share their stories in a dialogical chorus that can offer the best chance of respecting all the persons involved in a case.[15]

In turn, for the narrative approach, relational virtues such as empathetic listening and support are privileged. In the course of such privileging, these virtues are reworked to acknowledge and accommodate the narrative view that, in some senses, difference is irreducible. For example,

Howard Brody radically reconceives the moral demands of "empathy" in the following passage:

> In a culture that prizes autonomy and independence, we may fondly imagine that most people are whole and intact, unlike those who suffer from disease . . . Charity tends to assume that I start off whole and remain whole while I offer aid to the suffering. Empathy and testimony require a full awareness of my own vulnerability and radical incompleteness; to be with the suffering as a cohuman presence will require that I change. . . . Today I listen to the testimony of someone's suffering; tomorrow that person (or someone else) will be listening to my testimony of my own. Today I help to heal the sufferer by listening to and validating her story; tomorrow that sufferer will have helped to heal me, as her testimony becomes a model I can use to better make sense of and deal with my own suffering.[16]

On Brody's view, the demand of empathy does not require us to step into another's shoes in order to understand their pain. It does not presuppose that it is ever possible to fully understand another's pain. The other person is always "other" to us, their difference persists, resisting assimilation under the umbrella of mutual understanding. Instead, empathy demands that we bear witness to our own vulnerability and lack so that we stand not as whole to part or healthy to ill, but as a "cohuman presence." On this view, the health professional cannot offer patients the reassurance that they know and understand them, only the acknowledgement that they have listened and heard. On this view, too, no health professional is untouched by a patient's pain and vulnerability; there is professional engagement, not detachment.

Acknowledging that a narrative approach to ethical decision making is not without its critics, I suggest that the three tenets I have just outlined manage to foreground some key ethical concerns in the healthcare arena.[17] What is refreshing about this approach is that it reconceptualizes the ethical decision making process and introduces the idea that the aim of ethics is not, necessarily, to reduce discord, disunity, and disagreement. Moreover, hitherto, traditional ethical approaches have configured the ideal decision maker as a unified and autonomous self and have subsequently defined the task of ethics as the determination of universal principles to guide that agent's conduct. Narrative ethics, on the other hand, eschews the notion of autonomous selfhood in favor of an account that recognizes the intersubjective and contextual nature of decision making and focuses on the uniqueness of each ethically challenging situation rather than its fit with general rules.

WHY THE NARRATIVE SELF?

In the final analysis, we are left with a choice of metaphors that direct us toward the world and ourselves and offer us ways of framing our experience and behavior. To borrow Dennett's phrase, the metaphor of the narrative self is a "tool of thought" that is useful and worth taking seriously for a number of reasons.[18]

First, it makes sense for theorists coming from both naturalist and continental philosophical perspectives to understand the self as a narrative unity.

Second, narrativity is a very natural mode of representation for human beings, not least because it captures the interpretive nature of the human world and a cluster of important features of human life—for example, temporality and corporeality.

Third, in appealing to any number of different culturally available forms of human selfhood, the narrative model can accommodate a very wide range of human experiences of selfhood—from the very stable to the radically fragmented. This, I suggest, is a reason to accept rather than reject it as an appropriate metaphor for the self. I am reminded of a familiar phrase from Merleau-Ponty: "The contingency of all that exists and all that has value is not a little truth for which we have somehow or other to make room in some nook and cranny of the system: it is the condition of a metaphysical view of the world."[19] Equally, the variation in our experiences of selfhood is not something that can be accommodated by viewing some unstable forms as pathological expressions of "normal" selves, but rather, it is a condition of human life which any adequate theory of selfhood must take into account.

Fourth, while the narrative approach does not deliver the kind of self that is capable of moral agency in the usual sense, it forces a rethink of existing ethical frameworks and foregrounds communicative and contextual features of the moral realm.

Finally, the narrative approach to selfhood achieves

all of this without committing us to the idea that the self must have a direct referent or that, lacking such a referent, the self must be illusory.

NOTES TO CONCLUSION

1. As Kathleen Wilkes puts it, the term "person" is defined in terms of what we think human beings actually are and what we think people ought to be (Wilkes, *Real People*, p. 198).

2. For critical examinations of different narrative approaches to bioethics, see *Stories and their Limits, Narrative Approaches to Bioethics*, ed. Hilde Lindemann Nelson (London: Routledge, 1997) and Hilde Lindemann Nelson, *Damaged Identities, Narrative Repair* (New York: Cornell University Press, 2001), pp. 36–68. See also *Narrative Based Medicine*, ed. T. Greenhalgh and B. Hurwitz (London: BMJ Books, 1998), which insists on the need for clinical training in interpretative skills to improve the diagnosis and treatment of illness. For a short overview of the role of narrative theory in bioethics, see K. Montgomery Hunter, "Narrative," in *Encyclopedia of Bioethics*, ed. T. R. Warren (New York: Simon and Schuster Macmillan, 1995), pp. 1789–94.

3. Given the broad spectrum of narrative approaches and their recent appearance in the field of bioethics, I think it best to gather them loosely under the title of "narrative ethics." For a dissenting view, see A. Hudson Jones, "Narrative in Medical Ethics," in *Narrative based medicine*, pp. 217–24.

4. Martha C. Nussbaum, *Love's Knowledge* (New York: Oxford University Press, 1992) and *Poetic Justice: The Literary Imagination and Public Life* (Boston, MA: Beacon Press, 1995).

5. Albert Jonsen and Stephen Toulmin, *The Abuse of Casuistry* (Berkeley, CA: University of California Press, 1988); John Arras, "Getting Down to Cases: the Revival of Casuistry in Bioethics," *The Journal of Medicine and Philosophy* 16 (1991): 29-51.

6. Rita Charon, "Narrative Contributions to Medical Ethics: Recognition, Formulation, Interpretation, and Validation in the Practice of the Ethicist," in *A Matter of Principles?* ed. E. R. DuBose, R. P. Hamel and L. J. O'Connell (Valley Forge, PA: Trinity Press International, 1994), pp. 260-83.

7. Tod Chambers, *The Fiction of Bioethics: Cases as Literary Texts* (New York: Routledge, 1999). See also *American Journal of Bioethics* 1, no. 1 (2001) for a range of open peer commentaries on Chambers' book drawn from philosophy, sociology, literature, and medicine.

8. Howard Brody, *Stories of Sickness* (New Haven and London: Yale University Press, 1987); Arthur Frank, *The Wounded Storyteller: Body, Illness and Ethics* (Chicago: Chicago University Press, 1995); Alasdair MacIntyre, *After Virtue: a Study in Moral Theory*; Kathryn Montgomery Hunter, *Doctors' Stories: the Narrative Structure of Medical Knowledge* (Princeton: Princeton University Press, 1992); Nelson, *Damaged Identities, Narrative Repair.*

9. Brody, *Stories of Sickness*; Nelson, *Damaged Identities, Narrative Repair.*

10. Brody, *Stories of Sickness*, p. xiii.

11. Tom Beauchamp and James Childress, *Principles of Biomedical Ethics*, 5th ed. (Oxford: Oxford University Press, 2001), pp. 398-99. Following John Rawls, Beauchamp and Childress describe the weighing and balancing of principles, beliefs, and actions as a process of reflective equilibrium.

12. Ricoeur, *TN*3, pp. 246-47.

13. Council on Ethical and Judicial Affairs, *Surrogate deci-*

266   Conclusion

sion making, no. 119 (Chicago: American Medical Association, June 2001).

14. For further discussion about the relationship between narrative and substituted judgment, see M.G. Kuczewski, "Commentary, Narrative Views of Personal Identity and Substituted Judgment in Surrogate Decision Making," *Journal of Law, Medicine and Ethics* 27, no.1 (1999): 32–36.

15. A. Hudson Jones, "Narrative in Medical Ethics," p. 222.

16. Brody, *Stories of Sickness*, pp. 21–22.

17. For some of the standard criticisms of narrative ethics, see James Childress, "Narrative(s) Versus Norm(s)," in *Stories and their Limits*, ed. Hilde Lindemann Nelson (New York: Routledge, 1997), pp. 252–71; and K. D. Clouser, "Philosophy, Literature, and Ethics: Let the Engagement Begin," *Journal of Medicine and Philosophy* 21 (1996): 321–40. For a robust criticism of the narrative project as a whole and narrative ethics, in particular, see Galen Strawson, "Against Narrativity," *Ratio* 17, no. 4 (2004): 428–52.

18. Dennett, *CE*, p. 455.

19. Maurice Merleau-Ponty, *Sense and Non-Sense*, trans. Hubert L. Dreyfus and Patricia Allen Dreyfus (Evanston: Northwestern University Press, 1964), p. 96.

REFERENCES

Akins, Kathleen. "Lost the Plot? Reconstructing Dennett's Multiple Drafts Theory of Consciousness." *Mind and Language* 11, no. 1 (1996): 1–43.

Albright, Daniel. "Literary and Psychological Models of the Self." In *The Remembering Self, Construction and Accuracy in the Self-Narrative*, edited by Ulric Neisser and Robyn Fivush, 19–39. Cambridge: Cambridge University Press, 1994.

American Psychiatric Association. *Diagnostic and Statistical Manual of Mental Disorders*. 4th ed. Washington, DC, 1994.

Anderson, Pamela. "Re-reading Myth in Philosophy: Hegel, Ricoeur and Irigaray Reading Antigone." In *Paul Ricoeur and Narrative*, edited by Morny Joy, 51–68. Alberta: University of Calgary Press, 1997.

Arendt, Hannah. *The Human Condition*. Chicago: University of Chicago Press, 1958.

Aristotle. *Categories*. In *Complete Works of Aristotle* vol. 1, Bollingen Series LXXI, edited by Jonathan Barnes, 3–24. Princeton, NJ: Princeton University Press, 1984.

———. *De Interpretatione*. In *Complete Works of Aristotle* vol. 1, Bollingen Series LXXI, edited by Jonathan Barnes, 25–38. Princeton, NJ: Princeton University Press, 1984.

———. *Poetics*. In *Complete Works of Aristotle* vol. 2, Bollingen Series LXXI, edited by Jonathan Barnes, 2316–40. Princeton, NJ: Princeton University Press, 1984.

Arras John. "Getting Down to Cases: The Revival of Casuistry in Bioethics." *Journal of Medicine and Philosophy* 16 (1991): 29–51.

Baier, Annette C. *Postures of the Mind*. Minneapolis: University of Minnesota Press, 1985.

Barthes, Roland. "The Discourse of History." In *Comparative Criticism: A Year Book* vol. 3, edited by E. S. Schaffer, translated by Stephen Bann. Cambridge: Cambridge University Press, 1967.

———. *Image, Music, Text*, translated by Stephen Heath. Glasgow: Fontana/Collins, 1977.

Beauchamp, Tom, and James Childress. *Principles of Biomedical Ethics*, 5th ed. Oxford: Oxford University Press, 2001.

Beckett, Samuel. "Not I." In *Collected Shorter Plays: Samuel Beckett*. New York: Grove Press, 1984.

Blamey, Kathleen. "From the Ego to the Self: A Philosophical Itinerary." In *The Philosophy of Paul Ricoeur*, The Library of Living Philosophers XXII, edited by Lewis Edwin Hahn, 571-603. Chicago and La Salle, IL: Open Court, 1995.

Block, Ned. "What Is Dennett's Theory a Theory of?" *Philosophical Topics* 22, nos. 1 and 2 (1994): 23-40.

Boden, Margaret A. "Consciousness and Human Identity: An Interdisciplinary Perspective." In *Consciousness and Human Identity*, edited by John Cornwell, 1-20. Oxford: Oxford University Press, 1998.

Brison, Susan J. "Outliving Oneself: Trauma, Memory, and Personal Identity." In *Feminists Rethink the Self*, edited by Diana Tietzens Meyers, 12-39. Boulder, CO: Westview Press, 1997.

Brody, Howard. *Stories of Sickness*. New Haven, CT, and London: Yale University Press, 1987.

Bruner, Jerome. *In Search of Mind, Essays in Autobiography*. New York: Harper and Row, 1983.

———. *Actual Minds, Possible Worlds*. Cambridge, MA: Harvard University Press, 1986.

———. "The 'Remembered' Self." In *The Remembering Self,*

Construction and Accuracy in the Self-Narrative, edited by Ulric Neisser and Robyn Fivush, 19–39. Cambridge: Cambridge University Press, 1994.

Carr, David. *Time, Narrative and History*. Bloomington: Indiana University Press, 1986.

———. "Phenomenology and Fiction in Dennett." *International Journal of Philosophical Studies* 6, no. 3 (1998): 331–44.

Chalmers, David J. *The Conscious Mind: In Search of a Fundamental Theory*. Oxford: Oxford University Press, 1996.

Chambers, Tod. *The Fiction of Bioethics: Cases as Literary Texts*. New York: Routledge, 1999.

Changeux, Jean-Pierre, and Paul Ricoeur. *What Makes Us Think?* Princeton, NJ: Princeton University Press, 2000.

Charon, R. "Narrative Contributions to Medical Ethics: Recognition, Formulation, Interpretation, and Validation in the Practice of the Ethicist." In *A matter of principles?* 260–83.

Chatman, Seymour. *Story and Discourse: Narrative Structure in Fiction and Film*. Ithaca, NY: Cornell University Press, 1978.

Childress, James. "Narrative(s) Versus Norm(s)." In *Stories and Their Limits*, edited by Hilde Lindemann Nelson, 252–71. New York: Routledge, 1997.

Churchland, Paul M. *Scientific Realism and the Plasticity of Mind*. Cambridge, MA: Cambridge University Press, 1979.

———. *A Neurocomputational Perspective: The Nature of Mind and the Structure of Science*. Cambridge, MA: MIT Press, 1990.

Clouser, K. D. "Philosophy, Literature, and Ethics: Let the Engagement Begin." *Journal of Medicine and Philosophy* 21 (1996): 321–40.

Council on Ethical and Judicial Affairs. *Surrogate Decision Making*. Chicago: American Medical Association, no. 119 (June 2001).

Damasio, Antonio R. *Descartes' Error.* London: Macmillan/ Papermac, 1996.

———. *The Feeling of What Happens.* London: Vintage, 2000.

Dauenhauer, Bernard P. "Ricoeur and Political Identity." In *Paul Ricoeur and Narrative,* edited by Morny Joy, 129–40. Alberta: University of Calgary Press, 1997.

———. *Paul Ricoeur, The Promise and the Risk of Politics.* Lanham, MD: Rowman and Littlefield, 1998.

Dennett, Daniel C. "Are We Explaining Consciousness Yet?" *Cognition* 79, nos.1 and 2 (2001): 221–37.

———. "Back from the Drawing Board." In *Dennett and His Critics,* edited by Bo Dahlbom, 203–35. Oxford: Blackwell, 1993.

———. *Brainchildren.* London: Penguin, 1998.

———. *Brainstorms.* Sussex: Harvester Press, 1979.

———. *Consciousness Explained.* London: Penguin, 1991.

———. *Darwin's Dangerous Idea.* London: Penguin, 1995.

———. "Dennett and Carr Further Explained: An Exchange." Emory Cognition Project, Report no. 28, Department of Psychology, Emory University, April 1994. Also titled "Tiptoeing Past the Covered Wagons." http://cogprints.org/278 /00/tiptoe.htm (accessed August 14, 2006).

———. "The Fantasy of First-Person Science." *Third Draft* (March 1, 2001). http://ase.tufts.edu/cogstud/papers /chalmersdeb3dft.htm (accessed August 14, 2006).

———. "Get Real." *Philosophical Topics* 22, nos. 1 and 2 (1994): 505–68.

———. *The Intentional Stance.* Cambridge, MA: Bradford Books/MIT Press, 1987.

———. *Kinds of Minds.* London: Weidenfeld & Nicolson, 1996.

———. "The Message Is: There Is No Medium." *Philosophy and Phenomenological Research* 53, no. 4 (1993): 919–31.

———. "Murmurs in the Cathedral." Review of *The Emperor's*

New Mind, by Roger Penrose. *Times Literary Supplement* (September 29–October 5, 1989).

———. "The Origin of Selves." *Cogito* 21 (1989): 163–73.

———. "Our Vegetative Soul." Review of *Descartes' Error,* by Antonio Damasio. *Times Literary Supplement* (August 25, 1995), p. 34.

———. "Postmodernism and Truth." Paper delivered at World Congress of Philosophy (August 13, 1998). http://www .butterfliesandwheels.com/articleprint.php?num=13 (accessed August 14, 2006).

———. "Précis of Consciousness Explained." *Philosophy and Phenomenological Research* 53, no. 4 (1993): 889–92.

———. "Quining Qualia." In *Consciousness in Contemporary Science,* edited by A. J. Marcel and E. Bisiach, 42–77. Oxford: Clarendon Press, 1988.

———. "Real Consciousness." In *Consciousness in Philosophy and Cognitive Science,* edited by A. Revonsuo and M. Kamppinen, 55–63. Hillsdale, NJ; Lawrence Erlbaum, 1994.

———. "Self-Portrait." In *A Companion to the Philosophy of Mind,* edited by S. Guttenplan, 236–44. Oxford: Blackwell, 1994.

———. "Why Everyone is a Novelist." *Times Literary Supplement* 4, no. 459 (1988): 1016–29.

———. "With a Little Help from My Friends." In *Dennett's Philosophy, A Comprehensive Assessment,* edited by Don Ross, Andrew Brook, and David Thompson, 327–88. Cambridge, MA: MIT Press, 2000.

Derrida, Jacques. *A Derrida Reader: Between the Blinds,* edited by Peggy Kamuf. New York: Columbia University Press, 1991.

Descartes, René. *Oeuvres de Descartes,* 11 vols., edited by Charles Adam and Paul Tannery. Paris: Vrin, 1964–1974.

Dilthey, Wilhelm. "The Rise of Hermeneutics." *New Literary History* 3, no. 2 (Winter 1972): 229–44.

Eagle, M. "Psychoanalysis and 'Narrative Truth': A Reply to Spence." *Psychoanalysis and Contemporary Thought* 7, no. 4 (1984): 629–40.

Elliston, F. A., and P. McCormick, eds. *Husserl: Expositions and Appraisals*. Notre Dame, IN: University of Notre Dame Press, 1977.

Flanagan, Owen. *Consciousness Reconsidered*. Cambridge, MA: MIT Press, 1994.

———. *Self Expressions*. Oxford: Oxford University Press, 1996.

Fodor, James. "The Tragic Face of Narrative Judgement: Christian Reflections on Paul Ricoeur's Theory of Narrative." In *Paul Ricoeur and Narrative*, edited by Morny Joy, 153–73. Alberta: University of Calgary Press, 1997.

Fodor, Jerry A. *Psychosemantics: The Problem of Meaning in the Philosophy of Mind*. Cambridge, MA: Bradford Books/MIT Press, 1987.

Foster, John. *The Immaterial Self*. London: Routledge, 1991.

Foucault, Michel. *The Care of the Self, History of Sexuality*, vol.3, translated by Robert Hurley. London: Penguin, 1986.

———. *Discipline and Punish*, translated by A. M. Sheridan-Smith. London: Smith, Allen Lane, 1977.

———. *The History of Sexuality*, vol. 1, translated by Robert Hurley. London: Penguin, 1978.

———. "The Subject and Power." In *Michel Foucault: Beyond Structuralism and Hermeneutics*, edited by Hubert L. Dreyfus and Paul Rabinow. Chicago: University of Chicago Press, 1982.

———. "Technologies of the Self." In *Technologies of the Self*, edited by Luther H. Martin, Huck Gutman, and Patrick H. Hutton, 16–49. London: Tavistock Publications, 1988.

———. "Truth, Power, Self: An Interview with Michel Foucault." In *Technologies of the Self*, edited by Luther H. Martin,

Huck Gutman, and Patrick H. Hutton, 9–15. London: Tavistock Publications, 1988.

———. "What Is an Author?" In *Essential Works of Foucault* 2, edited by James D. Faubion, 205–27. New York: New Press, 1994.

Frank, Arthur. *The Wounded Storyteller: Body, Illness and Ethics*. Chicago: Chicago University Press, 1995.

Freud, Sigmund. "Mourning and Melancholia." In *On Metapsychology: The Theory of Psychoanalysis*, 251–68. London: Penguin, 1984.

———. "Remembering, Repeating and Working-Through." In *Standard Edition of the Complete Psychological Works of Sigmund Freud* 12, edited by James Strachey in collaboration with Anna Freud, 147–56. London: Hogarth Press, 1964.

———. "The Unconscious." In *Standard Edition of the Complete Psychological Works of Sigmund Freud* 14, edited by James Strachey in collaboration with Anna Freud. London: Hogarth Press, 1964.

Gadamer, Hans-Georg. *Truth and Method*. London: Sheed and Ward, 1975.

Gallagher, Shaun. "Philosophical Conceptions of the Self: Implications for Cognitive Science." *Trends in Cognitive Sciences* 4, no.1 (January, 2000): 14–21.

Gallagher, Shaun, and Jonathan Shear, eds. *Models of the Self.* New York: Imprint Academic, 1999.

Greenberg, Gary. "If a Self Is a Narrative: Social Constructionism in the Clinic." *Journal of Narrative and Life History* 5, no. 3 (1995): 269–83.

Greenhalgh, T., and B. Hurwitz, eds. *Narrative Based Medicine*. London: BMJ Books, 1998.

Greisch, Jean. "Testimony and Attestation." In *Paul Ricoeur, The Hermeneutics of Action,* edited by Richard Kearney, 81–98. London: Sage Publications, 1996.

Hardcastle, Valerie Gray. "A New Agenda for Studying Consciousness, Commentary on Puccetti on Split-Brain." *Psycoloquy* 4, no. 57 (1993). http://psycprints.ecs.soton.ac.uk/archive/00000351/ (accessed August 14, 2006).

Hartman, Heinz. "Psychoanalysis as a Scientific Theory." In *Psychoanalysis, Scientific Method and Philosophy*, edited by Sidney Hook, 3-37. New York: New York University Press, 1959.

Heidegger, Martin. *Being and Time*, translated by John Macquarrie and Edward Robinson. Oxford: Blackwell, 1973.

Hook, Sidney, ed. *Psychoanalysis, Scientific Method and Philosophy*. New York: New York University Press, 1959.

Humphrey, Nicholas, and Daniel Dennett. "Speaking for Our Selves." In Dennett, Daniel C. *Brainchildren*, 31-55. London: Penguin, 1998.

Hunter Montgomery, K. *Doctors' Stories: The Narrative Structure of Medical Knowledge*. Princeton, NJ: Princeton University Press, 1992.

———. "Narrative." In *Encyclopedia of Bioethics*, edited by T. R. Warren, 1789-94. New York: Simon and Schuster Macmillan, 1995.

Husserl, Edmund. *Cartesian Meditations*, translated by Dorion Cairns. The Hague: Martinus Nijhoff, 1960.

———. *The Crisis of European Sciences and Transcendental Phenomenology*, translated by David Carr. Evanston: Northwestern University Press, 1970.

———. *The Phenomenology of Time Consciousness*, translated by James S. Churchill. The Hague: Martinus Nijhoff, 1964.

James, William. "The Stream of Consciousness." In *Modern Philosophy of Mind*, edited by William Lyons, 3-23. London: Everyman, 1995.

Jones Hudson A. "Narrative in Medical Ethics." In *Narrative Based Medicine,* edited by T. Greenhalgh and B. Hurwitz, 217-24. London: BMJ Books, 1998.

Jonsen, Albert, and Stephen Toulmin. *The Abuse of Casuistry*. Berkeley: University of California Press, 1988.

Joy, Morny. "Writing as Repossession: The Narratives of Incest Victims." In *Paul Ricoeur and Narrative*, edited by Morny Joy, 35–49. Alberta: University of Calgary Press, 1997.

Kant, Immanuel. *Critique of Pure Reason*, translated by Norman Kemp Smith. New York: St. Martin's, 1995.

Kearney, Richard. "Narrative Imagination: Between Ethics and Poetics." In *Paul Ricoeur, The Hermeneutics of Action*, edited by Richard Kearney, 173–90. London: Sage Publications, 1996.

———. "Paul Ricoeur and the Hermeneutic Imagination." *Special Issue: The Narrative Path: The Later Works of Paul Ricoeur, Philosophy and Social Critics* 14, no. 2, edited by David M. Rasmussen and T. Peter Kemp. Cambridge, MA: MIT Press, 1988.

Kermode, Frank. *The Sense of an Ending: Studies in the Theory of Fiction*. London: Oxford University Press, 1966.

Kirk, Robert. "'The Best Set of Tools'? Dennett's Metaphors and the Mind-Body Problem." *Philosophical Quarterly* 43, no. 172 (1993): 334–43.

Kristeva, Julia. *In the Beginning Was Love: Psychoanalysis and Faith*, translated by A. Goldhammer. New York: Columbia University Press, 1987.

Kuczewski, M. G. "Commentary, Narrative Views of Personal Identity and Substituted Judgement in Surrogate Decision Making." *Journal of Law, Medicine and Ethics* 27, no.1 (1999): 32–36.

Lavine, Thelma. "Ricoeur and the Conflict of Interpretations." In *The Philosophy of Paul Ricoeur*, edited by Lewis Edwin Hahn, 169–88. Chicago and La Salle, IL: Open Court, 1995.

Locke, John. *An Essay concerning Human Understanding*, edited by Peter H. Nidditch. Oxford: Clarendon, 1975.

Lodge, David. *Nice Work*. London: Secker and Warberg, 1988.

Luria, Alexander Romanovich, *Higher Cortical Functions in Man*, translated by Basil Haigh. New York: Basic Books, 1980.

MacIntyre, Alasdair. *After Virtue: A Study in Moral Theory*. Notre Dame, IN: University of Notre Dame Press, 1981.

Madison, Gary B. "Ricoeur and the Hermeneutics of the Subject." In *The Philosophy of Paul Ricoeur*, edited by Lewis Edwin Hahn. 75–92. Chicago and La Salle, IL: Open Court, 1995.

McAdams, Dan P. "Introductory Commentary." *Journal of Narrative and Life History* 5, no. 3 (1995): 207–11.

———. *The Stories We Live By, Personal Myths and the Making of the Self*. New York: William Morrow and Co., 1993.

Merleau-Ponty, Maurice. *Phenomenology of Perception*, translated by Colin Smith. London: Routledge and Kegan Paul, 1981.

———. *Sense and Non-Sense*, translated by Hubert L. Dreyfus and Patricia Allen Dreyfus. Evanston: Northwestern University Press, 1964.

Miller, J. Hillis. *Ariadne's Thread: Story Lines*. New Haven, CT: Yale University Press, 1992.

———. *Reading Narrative*. Norman, OK: Oklahoma University Press, 1998.

Mink, Louis. "History and Fiction as Modes of Comprehension." *New Literary History* 1, no. 3 (Spring 1970): 541–58.

———. "Narrative Form as a Cognitive Instrument." In *The Writing of History: Literary Form and Historical Understanding*, edited by Robert H. Canary and Henry Kozicki, 143–44. Ontario: Madison Press, 1978.

Musil, Robert. *L'homme sans qualités*. Paris: Seuil, 1979.

Nagel, Ernest. "Methodological Issues in Psychoanalytic Theory." In *Psychoanalysis, Scientific Method and Philos-*

ophy, edited by Sidney Hook, 38–56. New York: New York University Press, 1959.

Nagel, Thomas. *A View from Nowhere*. Oxford: Oxford University Press, 1986.

———. "What Is It Like to Be a Bat?" *Philosophical Review* no. 4 (1974): 435–50.

Nelson, Hilde Lindemann. *Damaged Identities, Narrative Repair*. New York: Cornell University Press, 2001.

———. *Stories and Their Limits, Narrative Approaches to Bioethics*. London: Routledge, 1997.

Nietzsche, Friedrich W. "On Truth and Lies in a Nonmoral Sense." In *Philosophy and Truth: Selections from Nietzsche's Notebooks of the Early 1870s*, translated by Daniel Breazeale, 79–97. Atlantic Highlands, NJ: Humanities Press, 1979.

———. *Will to Power, Complete Works*, vol. 15, translated by Anthony M. Ludovici. Edinburgh: T. N. Fowlis, 1910.

Nussbaum, Martha C. *Love's Knowledge*. New York: Oxford University Press, 1992.

———. *Poetic Justice: The Literary Imagination and Public Life*. Boston: Beacon, 1995.

Olson, Eric T. "There Is No Problem of the Self." *Journal of Consciousness Studies* 5, nos. 5–6 (1998): 645–57.

Palmer, Richard E. *Hermeneutics*. Evanston: Northwestern University Press, 1969.

Parfit, Derek. "Personal Identity." *Philosophical Review* 80 (1971): 3–27.

———. *Reasons and Persons*. Oxford: Oxford University Press, 1984.

Polkinghorne, Donald E. "Narrative and Self-Concept." *Journal of Narrative and Life History* 1, nos. 2 and 3 (1991): 135–53.

Puccetti, Roland. "Dennett on the Split-Brain." *Psycoloquy* 4, no. 52

(1993). http://psycprints.ecs.soton.ac.uk/archive/00000377/ (accessed August 14, 2006).

———. "Narrative Richness as a Necessary Condition for the Self." *Psycoloquy* 5, no. 18 (1994). http://psycprints.ecs .soton.ac.uk/archive/00000377/ (accessed August 14, 2006).

———. "Two Brains, Two Minds? Wigan's Theory of Mental Duality." In *Self and Identity, Contemporary Philosophical Issues*, edited by Daniel Kolak and Raymond Martin. New York: Macmillan Publishing Company, 1991.

Reichenbach, Hans. *The Rise of Scientific Philosophy*. Berkeley: University of California Press, 1951.

Ricoeur, Paul. "Autonomie et Vulnerabilité." Paper presented at Seance Inaugurale du Seminaire de l'IHE, November 6, 1995. (Cited in Dauenhauer. *Paul Ricoeur, The Promise and the Risk of Politics*, 124.)

———. "Existence and Hermeneutics." In *The Conflict of Interpretations*, edited by Don Ihde, translated by Kathleen Blamey, 3–24. Evanston, IL: Northwestern University Press, 2007.

———. "Explanation and Understanding: On Some Remarkable Connections Among the Theory of the Text, Theory of Action, and Theory of History." In *The Philosophy of Paul Ricoeur: An Anthology of his Work*, edited by Charles E. Reagan and David Stewart, 149–66. Boston: Beacon, 1978.

———. *Fallible Man*, translated by Charles A. Kelbley. New York: Fordham University Press, 1986.

———. *Freedom and Nature: The Voluntary and the Involuntary*, translated by Erazim V. Kohak. Evanston, IL: Northwestern University Press, 1966.

———. "From Metaphysics to Moral Philosophy." *Philosophy Today* 39, no. 4 (1996): 443–58.

———. "From Psychoanalysis to the Question of the Self, or

Thirty Years of Philosophical Work." In *Critique and Conviction: Conversation with François Azouvi and Marc de Launay*, translated by Kathleen Blamey, 68-94. Cambridge, MA: Polity Press, 1998.

———. *Freud and Philosophy: An Essay on Interpretation*, translated by Denis Savage. New Haven, CT: Yale University Press, 1970.

———. *History and Truth*, translated by Charles A. Kelbley. Evanston, IL: Northwestern University Press, 1965.

———. "The Human Being as the Subject Matter of Philosophy." *Philosophy and Social Criticism* 14, no. 2 (1988): 203-15.

———. "Imagination, Testimony and Trust, A dialogue with Paul Ricoeur." In *Questioning Ethics,* edited by Richard Kearney and Mark Dooley, 12-17. London: Routledge, 1999.

———. "Intellectual Autobiography." In *Philosophy of Paul Ricoeur*, edited by Lewis Edwin Hahn, translated by Kathleen Blamey, 3-54. Chicago and La Salle, IL: Open Court, 1995.

———. *The Just,* translated by David Pellauer. Chicago: University of Chicago Press, 2000.

———. "Life in Quest of Narrative." In *On Paul Ricoeur, Narrative and Interpretation*, edited by David Wood, 20-33. London: Routledge, 1991.

———. "Memory and Forgetting." In *Questioning Ethics,* edited by Richard Kearney and Mark Dooley, 5-11. London: Routledge, 1999.

———. "Narrative Identity." *Philosophy Today* (Spring 1991): 73-81.

———. *Oneself as Another*, translated by Kathleen Blamey. Chicago: University of Chicago Press, 1992.

———. "On Interpretation." In *Philosophy in France Today*,

edited by A. Montefiore, 175–97. Cambridge, MA: Cambridge University Press, 1983.

———. "The Question of Proof in Freud's Writings." In *Hermeneutics and the Human Sciences*, edited and translated by John B. Thompson, 247–73. Cambridge, MA: Cambridge University Press, 1981.

———. "Reply to Dabney Townsend." In *The Philosophy of Paul Ricoeur*, edited by Lewis Edwin Hahn, 212. Chicago and La Salle, IL: Open Court, 1995.

———. "Reply to G. B. Madison." In *The Philosophy of Paul Ricoeur*, edited by Lewis Edwin Hahn, 93. Chicago and La Salle, IL: Open Court, 1995.

———. "A Response by Paul Ricoeur." In *Paul Ricoeur and Narrative*, edited by Morny Joy, xxxix-xliv. Alberta: University of Calgary Press, 1997.

———. *The Rule of Metaphor: Multi-disciplinary Studies of the Creation of Meaning in Language*, translated by Robert Czerny. Toronto: University of Toronto Press, 1977.

———. "The Task of Hermeneutics." In *Hermeneutics and the Human Sciences*, edited and translated by John B. Thompson, 43–62. Cambridge, MA: Cambridge University Press, 1981.

———. *Time and Narrative*, 3 vols., translated by Kathleen Blamey and David Pellauer. Chicago: University of Chicago Press, 1984–1988.

Rorty, Richard. *Contingency, Irony, and Solidarity*. Cambridge, MA: Cambridge University Press, 1989.

———. "Holism, Intrinsicality, and the Ambition of Transcendence." In *Dennett and his Critics*, edited by Bo Dahlbom, 184–202. London: Blackwell, 1993.

Ryle, Gilbert. *The Concept of Mind*. London: Hutchinson, 1949.

Sacks, Oliver. *The Man Who Mistook His Wife for a Hat*. London: Duckworth, 1985.

Scriven, Michael. "The Experimental Investigation of Psychoanalysis." In *Psychoanalysis, Scientific Method and Philosophy*, edited by Sidney Hook, 226-51. New York: New York University Press, 1959.

Searle, John R. "Consciousness Denied: Daniel Dennett's Account." In *The Mystery of Consciousness*, edited by John Searle, 98-131. London: Granta Publications, 1998.

———. *Speech Acts*. Cambridge, MA: Cambridge University Press, 1969.

———. *The Rediscovery of the Mind*. Cambridge, MA: MIT Press, 1992.

Spence, Donald P. "Narrative Appeal vs Historical Validity." *Contemporary Psychoanalysis* 25, no. 3 (1989): 517-24.

———. "Narrative Persuasion." *Psychoanalysis and Contemporary Thought* 6, no. 3 (1983): 457-81.

———. *Narrative Truth and Historical Truth*. New York: Norton, 1982.

Sperry, R. W. "Hemisphere Deconnection and Unity in Conscious Awareness." In *Self and Identity, Contemporary Philosophical Issues*, edited by Daniel Kolak and Raymond Martin. New York: Macmillan, 1991.

Sprinker, Michael. "Fictions of the Self: The End of Autobiography." In *Autobiography: Essays Theoretical and Critical*, edited by James Olney. Princeton, NJ: Princeton University Press, 1980.

Strawson, Galen. "The Self." *Journal of Consciousness Studies* 4, nos. 5-6 (1997): 405-28.

———. "The Self and the Sesmet." *Journal of Consciousness Studies* 6, no. 4 (1999): 99-135.

———. "Against Narrativity." *Ratio* 17, no. 4 (2004): 428-52.

Strawson, P. F. *Individuals*. London: Menthuen, 1959.

Taylor, Charles. *The Explanation of Behaviour*. London: Routledge and Kegan Paul, 1954.

———. *Sources of the Self: The Making of Modern Identity*. Cambridge, MA: Harvard University Press, 1989.

———. "What Is Human Agency?" In *The Self: Psychological and Philosophical Issues*, edited by T. Mischel. Oxford: Blackwell, 1977.

Thompson, David L. "Phenomenology and Heterophenomenology: Husserl and Dennett on Reality and Science." In *Dennett's Philosophy, A Comprehensive Assessment*, edited by Don Ross, Andrew Brook, and David Thompson. Cambridge, MA: MIT Press, 2000.

Walker, Margaret Urban. *Moral Understandings*. London: Routledge, 1998.

———. "Picking Up Pieces, Lives, Stories, and Integrity." In *Feminists Rethink the Self*, edited by Diana Tietzens Meyers, 62–84. Boulder, CO: Westview Press, 1997.

White, Hayden. *The Content of the Form: Narrative Discourse and Historical Representation*. Baltimore, MD: John Hopkins University Press, 1987.

———. "The Metaphysics of Narrativity." In *On Paul Ricoeur, Narrative and Interpretation*, edited by David Wood, 140–59. London: Routledge, 1991.

———. "The Value of Narrativity in the Representation of Reality." In *On Narrative*, edited by W. J. T. Mitchell. Chicago: University of Chicago Press, 1981.

White, Richard. *Remembering Ahanagran, Storytelling in a Family's Past*. New York: Hill and Wang, 1998.

Wigan, Arthur Ladbroke. A *New View of Insanity: The Duality of the Mind Proved by the Structure, Functions and Diseases*. London: Longmans, 1884.

Wilkes, Kathleen. "Know Thyself." *Journal of Consciousness Studies* 5, no. 2 (1998): 153–65.

———. *Real People*. Oxford: Clarendon, 1994.

Williams, Bernard. "Descartes." In *The Concise Encyclopaedia of Western Philosophy and Philosophers*, edited by J. O. Urmson and Jonathan Rée, 72–78. London: Unwin Hyman, 1989.

———. *Problems of the Self*. Cambridge, MA: Cambridge University Press, 1973.

Wittgenstein, Ludwig. *Tractatus Logico-Philosophicus*, translated by D. F. Pears and B. F. McGuinness. London: Routledge, 1961.

Woolf, Virginia. *Mrs. Dalloway*. San Diego, CA: Harcourt, 1981.

———. *Orlando*. Oxford: Oxford University Press, 1998.

INDEX